TANTE MARIE BOOK OF
FRENCH COOKING

TANTE MAR

FRENCH

IE BOOK OF
COOKING

BERYL CHILDS AND SUE ALEXANDER

Macdonald

For John and Tony

A Macdonald Book

Copyright © Quarto Publishing Ltd, 1985

First published in Great Britain in 1985
by Macdonald & Co (Publishers) Ltd
London & Sydney
A member of BPCC plc

British Library Cataloguing in Publication Data

Childs, Beryl
Tante Marie book of French cooking.
1. Cookery, French
I. Title II. Alexander, Sue
641.3'00944 TX719

ISBN 0-356-10925-9

This book was designed and produced by
Quarto Publishing Ltd
The Old Brewery, 6 Blundell Street
London N7 9BH

Senior Editor Tessa Rose
Editor Sue Fleming

Art Editor Nick Clark
Design David Brown
Photographer Paul Forrester
Cartography Ellie King

Art Director Alastair Campbell
Editorial Director Jim Miles

Typeset by Facsimile, Coggeshall, Essex
Colour origination by Universal Colour Scanning Ltd,
Hong Kong
Printed by LeeFung Asco Printers Ltd, Hong Kong

Macdonald & Co (Publishers) Ltd
Maxwell House
74 Worship Street
London EC2A 2EN

CONTENTS

INTRODUCTION

When we were asked to write a book on French cookery, we were determined not to simply lift recipes from the archives of the Tante Marie School. This would have been all too easy. We preferred instead to present a selection of recipes from the regions, along with a few of the classic recipes of French cuisine, and in such a form that they could be successfully prepared and presented in a domestic kitchen. French cookery tends to frighten many, but we feel that our methods, perfected over many years of teaching, can help, enlighten and benefit all cooks, whether beginners or experts. The emphasis of the book, therefore, is on the recipes — basic, classic and regional — and they are laid out simply and clearly.

No two French chefs will agree on a precise definition of 'haute cuisine', but there are certain French dishes that come immediately to mind when haute cuisine is mentioned. It is some of these that we have chosen to include in the classic section. These dishes tend to be rather more elaborate in both preparation and presentation than those from the regions, but we have written them in such a way that the prospect of tackling them should not seem too daunting.

As we are covering French regional and classic cookery, it would be wrong for us to ignore 'la nouvelle cuisine'. This way of cooking and presenting food is either loved or hated by members of the profession. There is no doubt that the food looks most attractive when it is served — it almost looks as though an artist has been at work — but there must be more than 'eye appeal' to satisfy the diner. The flavours are usually delicate and fresh, but the portion sizes are very meagre. It is not necessary to have special recipes to create this kind of food, and perhaps the best compromise can be achieved by adapting conventional recipes and serving them artistically arranged in individual portions on plain plates.

Those with some cookery knowledge may be able to follow the recipes without referring to other sections in the book, but it is most important that the novice cook should be familiar with the various techniques and processes to which we refer.

The categorization of recipes is by no means rigid, as some of the first courses would be suitable to serve as a light main course and smaller portions of some of the main courses or vegetables could be served as a first course. So long as you follow the estimation of average portions that is suggested within the book, you can adapt the recipes accordingly.

This book does not aim to cover the whole enormous field of French cookery, but should stand as an introduction to its joys, from the simplest regional dish to the heights of haute cuisine. We also include guidance on many other aspects: to buying and storing ingredients, how to plan menus, how to understand many basic techniques and cookery terms. We wish you success, and hope that our ideas will inspire you to share our love of France and its food.

A tradition which has been carried through the ages — and is still an important part of everyday life in France (far right) — is the daily trip to the boulangerie or bakers to pick up the freshly baked bread.

THE REGIONS

Geographical, cultural and climatic differences between the various regions have been among the factors responsible for the development of several distinct culinary styles, all of which provide a rich source of recipes for the home cook.

ILE DE FRANCE AND THE NORTH

Paris has always been a magnet for provincial immigrants seeking their fortunes, many of whom brought the cooking traditions of their native regions with them. It is often said that Paris does not possess any culinary specialities that are peculiarly her own. This may be so, but there are numerous recipes given the title 'à la Parisienne', not least those small Italian dumplings made of choux paste, Gnocchi à la Parisienne. The soupe à l'oignon served at the old Les Halles market in Paris could probably claim to be completely Parisian in connotation if not origin, as could the cake Paris-Brest, which was created at the turn of the century to commemorate the Paris-Brest bicycle race.

The finest sole and other fish are transported from Dieppe and other northern ports; fresh fruit and vegetables arrive daily from the market gardens of the Ile de France and the Champagne region — asparagus from Argenteuil, which provides an elegant garnish to Filet de Sole Ile de France, and strawberries from Vaugiraud (delicious with Crème Chantilly, the rich whipped cream created in honour of the Duc de Condé who owned a château at Chantilly in the heart of the Ile de France). The comparative closeness of the border with Belgium has provided many Flemish influences, notably that of the Carbonnade de boeuf flamande.

One cannot leave this region without mentioning two other notable products: the Brie cheese, of which there are many varieties and that wonderful bubbly wine, champagne (perfected by the monk Dom Perignon towards the end of the seventeenth century), a bottle of which turns any meal into an occasion.

France is famous for its bread. Every village and town has its own boulangerie. The long sticks known as baguettes may be copied throughout the world in shape, but there is no comparison when it comes to the taste, smell and flavour of the real thing.

BRITTANY

Brittany may not produce a spectacular or extraordinary cuisine but Breton dishes are simple in tradition and based on raw materials of very fine quality.

It is a windswept province, surrounded on three sides by the sea, and this has inevitably influenced the agriculture and the cooking. Globe artichokes and cauliflowers grow in abundance around Roscoff where the soil is poor due to salt spray and strong sea winds and, therefore, unsuitable for anything but crops that cling to the ground.

The salt marsh lamb from the bay of Mont St Michel is used in that famous dish Gigot aux haricots à la Bretonne. Around the coastline — which is one of the most dangerous in the world — mussels, clams, scallops and spider crabs are plentiful. Other fish to look for are mackerel, which can be sampled in Quimper served cold with a mustard sauce, sweet, firm monkfish served 'à l'Armoricaine' (after the ancient name of Brittany) and skate with black butter sauce.

Brittany is also famous for its butter, which is used in a number of cakes. Douarnenez is the home of the famous butter cake, Kuign Aman, similar in texture to croissant but much sweeter.

All over the region is found the equally delicious Far Breton — a combination of a sweet batter and fruit. The smallest towns and villages in Brittany have at least one crêperie where wafer-thin crêpes or galettes are served with a variety of fillings as a main course, dessert or snack at any time of the day.

The only notable Breton vineyards are those around the city of Nantes, near the mouth of the Loire. Muscadet is the chief variety and this dry, crisp white wine complements the local shellfish perfectly. Another local white wine, Gros Plant Nantais, has more bite than Muscadet and is a refreshing summer drink. However, the principal drink in this area is cider, the best examples of which come from Fouesnant and Beg-meil.

Brittany is surrounded by the sea and, naturally, because of this, seafood of every description is found in abundance. It is hardly surprising that the local cuisine makes full use of its raw materials. At the Cancale oyster beds (above), the women are sorting the oysters at low tide.

ANJOU AND THE LOIRE

The Loire river and its tributaries supply the freshwater fish that are part of many famous regional dishes, Saumon poché au beurre blanc for example. Along the banks of these rivers the fertile soil is covered with vineyards that produce white wines which are among the best in France. They are made from the Chenin Blanc grape and include Muscadet, Vouvray, Sauvennière and Saumur. After Champagne the sparkling wines of the Loire are the most famous in France. Made by the 'methode champenoise', they can be sold as Saumur Mousseux or, under slightly more rigorous regulations, as Crémant de Loire.

Prunes are used a great deal in the Loire Valley, their popularity dating from the First Crusades when plums were brought from Damascus. They are used in both savoury and sweet dishes: the unusual recipe Côte de porc aux pruneaux can be sampled in many restaurants in Tours, and combines the prunes of the area with Vouvray, which is also used for cooking poultry.

The area is famous for its market gardens, many of which produce a variety of pears — Williams-Duchesse, Jeanne d'Arc and Anjou — as well as plums which are used to make tarts, pies and many other beautiful desserts.

The gastronome Curnonsky was born at Angers, and may well have enjoyed some of the fresh cream cheese desserts, known as Crémets, which are served with sugar or a fruit purée.

THE LYONNAIS

Lyon has the reputation of being a leading gastronomic centre, and the most obvious reason for this is its situation and accessibility to some of the best raw materials and foods in France. It is a neighbour of Burgundy and, therefore, takes advantage of the Charolais beef and Bresse poultry;

and it rears many quality pigs which form the basis of a thriving and famed charcuterie. It is near Dauphiné, which was one of the first regions to successfully cultivate potatoes in the seventeenth century. Saucisson en brioche, usually made from the sausages special to the region, is as well known in the Lyonnais as a sausage roll in England, or a hot dog in the United States, but no further comparison is possible. Lyonnais cooks do not admit that onions play an overwhelming role in their cooking. They do, however, agree that onions add a certain vitality to the cooking of potatoes. Pommes de terre Lyonnaise, which consists of sautéed potatoes and simple fried onions, is a prime example of this.

Another speciality is Blanquette d'agneau des bords du Rhône — an unusual lamb dish garnished with some of the many fresh vegetables that are grown on the Lyonnais plains. Sweet chestnuts gathered from the many chestnut trees in the region, combined with the chocolate which was first developed by the confiseurs from Italy in the eighteenth century, form the basis of many desserts, such as Mousse au chocolat et aux marrons.

The city of Lyon is ideally placed for the enjoyment of good wine, with the vineyards of Beaujolais to the north-west and those of the Rhône to the south. In the immediate area, although not as distinguished as the wines of Burgundy, Côteaux de Lyonnais and Vin du Lyonnais are made in the Beaujolais style.

Once the oysters have been sorted they are put into wire baskets (below), and sold. As well as being a main part of the Bretons' diet, seafood is also one of their main sources of income.

PROVENCE

Provence could be called the herb garden of France, for nowhere else can one breathe air that is perfumed by a multitude of wild herbs — oregano, fennel, sage, savory, thyme and rosemary. Herbs are a major business here and are as characteristic to the Provençal cuisine as are the rich and strong flavours of garlic (in the garlic mayonnaise, aioli) and anchovy, appearing in dishes such as Anchoiade, Tapenade and Pissaladière (which takes its name from 'pissala' or 'pissalat' — a purée of small fish such as anchovies — not from its Italian cousin, the pizza). The tomatoes used in Pissaladière are also characteristic to the area as are sweet peppers, saffron and olive oil, and most of these feature in the famous local dish Ratatouille — a vegetable stew.

The one-time profusion of Mediterranean fish formed the basis of many fish dishes, notably Bouillabaisse, but there are also meat and poultry dishes such as the long-simmered beef daubes and sautés of chicken.

Provençal cuisine includes few desserts, as fruits, particularly the locally grown figs and melons, are more popular as the finale to a meal.

One of the most famous areas in the south is Provence. Set inland from the Mediterranean it enjoys the luxury of long hot sunny days making eating outdoors (left) an enjoyable part of everyday life.

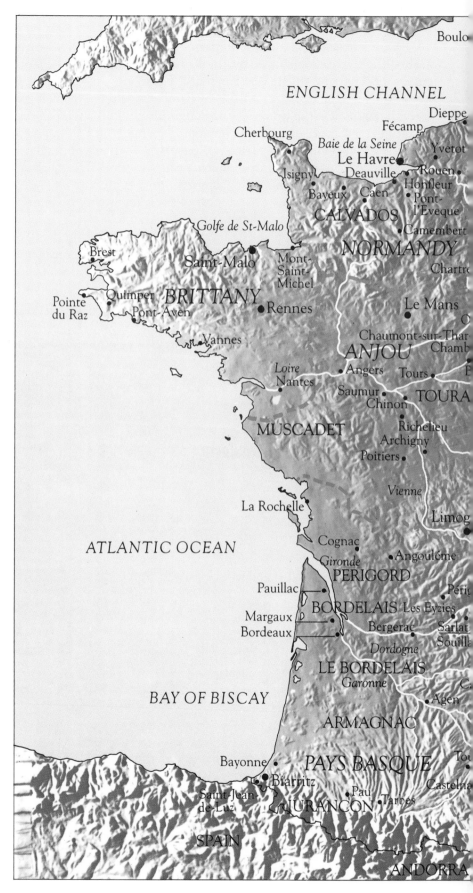

In this map of France we have shown the main regional cuisine and wine areas which we have talked about and will be covering in this book.

Key: Areas shaded in yellow denote wine regions.

ENGLISH CHANNEL

Boulo

Dieppe
Fécamp
Cherbourg
Baie de la Seine
Yvetot
Le Havre
Isigny
Deauville
Rouen
Honfleur
Bayeux
Caen
Pont-
l'Eveque
CALVADOS
Camembert
Golfe de St-Malo
NORMANDY
Chartre
Saint-Malo
Mont-
Brest
Saint-
Michel
Le Mans
Quimper
BRITTANY
Chaumont-sur-Thar
Pointe
Pont-Aven
Rennes
ANJOU
Chamb
du Raz
Vannes
Angers
Tours
TOURA
Loire
Saumur
Nantes
Chinon
Richelieu
MUSCADET
Archigny
Poitiers
Vienne
La Rochelle
Limog
ATLANTIC OCEAN
Cognac
Angoulême
Gironde
PERIGORD
Pauillac
BORDELAIS
Les Eyzies
Périg
Margaux
Bergerac
Sarlat
Bordeaux
Souilla
Dordogne
LE BORDELAIS
Garonne
BAY OF BISCAY
Agen
ARMAGNAC
Bayonne
PAYS BASQUE
Tou
Biarritz
Castelna
Saint-Jean
Pau
Tarbes
de-Luz
JURANCON
SPAIN
ANDORRA

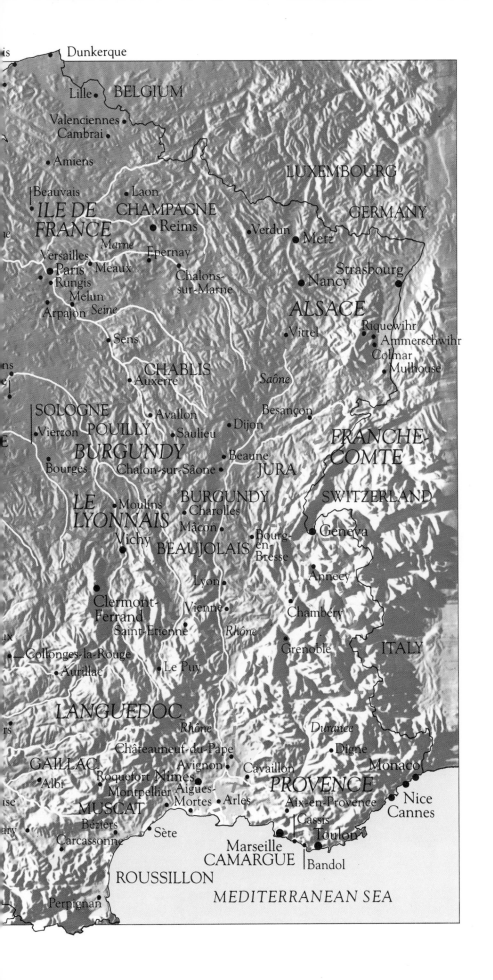

Dunkerque

Lille • BELGIUM

Valenciennes •
Cambrai •

• Amiens

LUXEMBOURG

Beauvais • • Laon
ILE DE   CHAMPAGNE   GERMANY
FRANCE   • Reims   • Verdun   • Metz

        Marne   • Epernay   Strasbourg
Versailles •   • Meaux   Chalons-   • Nancy
• Paris   sur-Marne
• Rungis   ALSACE
   Melun   Riquewihr •
Arpajon •   Seine   • Vittel   • Ammerschwihr
                                              Colmar •
        • Sens   • Mulhouse

        CHABLIS   Saône
           • Auxerre
                              • Besançon
SOLOGNE   • Avallon   FRANCHE
• Vierzon POUILLY • Saulieu   • Dijon COMTE
BURGUNDY   • Beaune
• Bourges   Chalon-sur-Sâone •   JURA   SWITZERLAND

LE   • Moulins   BURGUNDY
LYONNAIS   • Charolles
           Mâcon •   Bourg-   • Geneva
• Vichy   BEAUJOLAIS   en-
                               Bresse
                              • Annecy
          Lyon •
Clermont-
Ferrand   Vienne •   • Chambéry
  • Saint-Etienne   Rhône
                         • Grenoble   ITALY
Collonges-la-Rouge •
  • Aurillac   • Le Puy

LANGUEDOC
              Rhône   Durance
                                • Digne
GAILLAC   Châteauneuf-du-Pape •
• Albi   Roquefort Nîmes • Avignon •   • Cavaillon   • Monaco
       Montpellier • Aigues-   PROVENCE   • Nice
MUSCAT   • Mortes   • Arles   Aix-en-Provence •   Cannes
  Béziers •   Cassis
• Carcassonne   • Sète   • Toulon
              Marseille
       CAMARGUE   Bandol
ROUSSILLON
       • Perpignan   MEDITERRANEAN SEA

13

Provence also grows grapes, both for the table and for wine — the best known of which is Côte de Provence, which comes in red, white and rosé (the latter the most popular in the sophisticated resorts along the Mediterranean).

FRANCHE-COMTE

The Franche-Comté, the Alpine area along the borders with Switzerland and Italy, is above all dairy country. Milk is made into one of the region's main exports, the French version of Gruyère cheese, but Emmenthal, Tomme de Savoie and Reblochon are also highly regarded. Gruyère cheese plays its part in many of the dishes characteristic of the region, above all a fondue which is usually associated with Swiss cuisine.

A variety of excellent food is produced in this province. The most famous dish to use the potatoes, milk and eggs of the region is Gratin Dauphinoise of which there are numerous variations.

The mountainous terrain supports a great deal of game — partridge, pheasant and guinea fowl. Fish too is found in abundance. Trout come from the River Isère which flows through Grenoble, and pike from the Rhône are made into feather-light quenelles, served in Nantua with a pink crayfish sauce.

Walnut trees are grown here too, particularly in the Dauphiné around Grenoble, and the nuts are used in salads, sauces and baking, their oil lending an unmistakable flavour to salad dishes.

There is a strong Italian influence throughout Savoy and Dauphiné. It

Everyone in France takes eating very seriously, especially Sunday lunch. At Château Prepavin (below), the whole family sits down to enjoy the wide variety of excellent food which is produced in this area.

was the Romans who first planted the famous vines and fruit trees. The Dauphiné wines belong to the full bodied reds of the Rhône, which are at their best in vintages such as Châteauneuf du Pape and Hermitage.

NORMANDY

The cuisine of Normandy is regarded by many as one of the best in all the provinces of France. This is readily understandable when one considers that Normandy produces excellent butter and cream, and that butter and cream are used in all the characteristic dishes of the region named 'à la Normande'. The rich milk of Normandy is made into some of the finest French cheeses — among them Camembert, Pont l'Evêque, Livarot and Neufchâtel. Faisan à la vallée d'Auge, named after the valley of the River Auge, is a typical example of Norman fare and contains butter, cream, cider and apples.

Apples spring immediately to mind when the cookery of Normandy is mentioned, and feature prominently in the numerous apple tarts to be found in pâtisseries and restaurants throughout the region. The local cider, too, is much in evidence. Stronger and drier than the English variety, it is also distilled into the spirit Calvados, which not only plays an important part in a number of Norman dishes but is often served during the meal itself to aid digestion.

The rocky coast of Normandy provides an abundance of sea food. Dieppe is the major port, the nearest to Paris, and dishes taking its name — 'à la Dieppoise' — contain mussels, shrimps and other sea food. The

Although the butter and cream of Normandy is considered by many to be the finest available, the region is far better known for its apples (left). It is from these apples that the famous apple brandy named Calvados is distilled.

No kitchen in France would be complete without its string of garlic. It is one of the most important ingredients of all French cookery, throughout every region.

small mussels of Dieppe are, in fact, considered to be some of the sweetest and most flavourful in all of France and, characteristically, are often cooked in cider instead of wine, or in a cream sauce.

BURGUNDY

'Some have built a hearth in their kitchen, but the Dukes of Burgundy, they have made a kitchen from their hearth.' So said the gastronome Curnonsky about the Duke of Burgundy who, in the fifteenth century, extended his kitchen to form his banqueting hall as well. Many of the most famous dishes of French cuisine have their origins in Burgundy — Coq au vin, Boeuf à la bourguignonne, and even gougères are thought to have originated here.

The region itself is rich in top quality foods and contains just about everything for the cook. In Bresse, south of Dijon, some of the finest chickens in France are bred which, combined with one of the great wines of the area, produce a coq au vin fit for a king. The Charolais country has given its name to the famous breed of beef cattle: the meat can be mild and sometimes tough, so it benefits from the traditional, long slow simmering characteristic of Boeuf à la bourguignonne. (The cubes of bacon or salt pork, mushrooms and baby onions used in this dish are the major pointers to a Burgundian dish.)

In the heart of the province there once was an abundance of wild quail but nowadays most quail here and elsewhere are farmed like chickens. The snails of Burgundy are famed for their succulence throughout the world. Served with the delicious Beurre à la bourguignonne, a powerful garlic butter, their flavour cannot be surpassed.

The city of Dijon has some specialities of its own. One is the mustard which is quite rightly considered the best in France, and which is included in dishes called 'à la dijonnaise'. Another is Cassis, a blackcurrant liqueur used not only to flavour many desserts, but also as the base of the white wine aperitif known as Kir (named after Canon Kir, Mayor of Dijon and hero of the Resistance who died in 1968).

Burgundy is most famous for its wines, both red and white. Its white wines are classic: from around Beaune come Meursault and Corton-Charlemagne; from the north there is the highly individual Chablis; and from the upper Loire come the more perfumed Sancerre and Pouilly Fumé. Red Burgundies vary in depth and concentration of flavour, and range from the heavy Chambertin of the north to the fruity Beaujolais of the south.

ALSACE AND LORRAINE

The quiche, whose name is now sadly attached to many open tarts with dubious fillings, has its home in Alsace and Lorraine. Its name is derived from the German 'küchen' or cake and should conjure a picture of a rich egg custard with ham, bacon or leeks in a crisp pastry case. In true Alsatian style, this is sometimes translated into a fruit pie, using the Quetsche plums, apricots or Montmorency cherries of the region.

On the most easterly edge of France, the region's major border is that with Germany, and many foods and dishes are reminiscent of those of Germany. Choucroûte is the French version of the German sauerkraut, and can be anything from an accompaniment to a meal in itself. The goose, for which choucroûte is a favoured accompaniment, is most valued for its liver, a foie gras that rivals that of Périgord.

In the Middle Ages the diet of the peasants and artisans of the region was austere and in winter bread was the staple food with some dried peas, beans and lentils, a few green vegetables being added in summer. It is, therefore, hard to believe that in 1560 Sebastian Stosskopf was capturing in his still-life paintings the beauty of a Pâté en croûte sliced through clearly, showing the inside with its selection of meats and game.

Alsace is famous for its rich Kugelhopf and some delicious fruit and custard flans, but it is Lorraine that is especially associated with sweet things: macaroons and chocolate gâteaux from Nancy, Madeleines from Commercy.

Alsace has one cheese of note, the Munster, but it is rich in vineyards which produce the distinctive wines of the area, such as Rieslings, Gewürztraminers and Tokay d'Alsace — some say the perfect accompaniment to the region's foie gras.

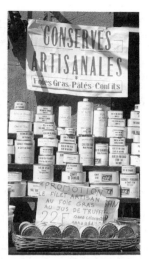

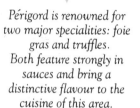

Périgord is renowned for two major specialities: foie gras and truffles. Both feature strongly in sauces and bring a distinctive flavour to the cuisine of this area.

PAYS BASQUE AND THE SOUTH-WEST

The Pays Basque, in the extreme south of France, lies between the Pyrenees and the Bay of Biscay. There are not a great number of local specialities, but those to be found are full of flavour. One typical example is the Bayonne ham. This is dry-cured to be eaten raw, or it can add its flavour to many fish dishes, as well as mousses. A classic example of Basquaise cooking is Pipérade — a mixture of ham, garlic, tomatoes, sweet peppers and creamy scrambled egg.

Further north is the city of Agen, known as the prune centre of France, and around here prunes are found in numerous local dishes, both savoury and sweet, ranging from Oie farcie aux pruneaux to Turban d'Agen, a creamy rice ring filled with prunes cooked in red wine. Other fruits, such as the cherries to accompany goose and for Clafoutis, are widely grown in the south-west, as are Charentais melons.

Further north still, in the Périgord, the particular specialities are the livers of force-fed geese (foie gras), and truffles (a fungus which grows at the root of oak and hazel trees), which contribute their flavour to most sauces and dishes labelled 'à la Périgourdine'.

The area around Bordeaux is the world's largest fine-wine region, producing many excellent whites and reds — including the vintage clarets known and prized throughout the world — and from here also come cognac, armagnac and marc.

LANGUEDOC AND THE CENTRE

West of Provence, the Languedoc shares many of its characteristic flavourings — notably garlic and anchovy — as well as a long coastline on the Mediterranean. It also borders on Spain, and many Spanish (as well as Arab) influences are obvious in the Languedoc cuisine, for

17

Truffles (right, are a fungus found growing on the roots of oak and hazel trees. They are considered a great delicacy, which is reflected in the price one has to pay for them. Poultry farming (below), has been popular all over France since the middle ages. Chicken especially has been a favourite with many French chefs, creating over the years such famous dishes as Coq au vin.

example, partridge cooked 'à la Catalane'. But the most famous dish of the province is Cassoulet. Three places claim to be its original home — Toulouse, Castelnaudary, and Carcassonne — and in each, although the dried white beans are the same, the meat content may differ.

Made from sheeps' milk, Roquefort cheese is one of the region's most renowned products and only in the limestone caves above the little town of Roquefort does the mould used in the development of the cheese flourish.

Other Languedoc specialities are Vichy carrots — which should properly be made only with the Massif Central water from the ancient spa town — chocolate truffles from Montpellier, and marrons glacés, made from the sweet chestnuts grown in the northern groves of the Ardèche. Montpellier is also famous for Beurre de Montpellier, which is a herb butter with mustard and anchovies.

Languedoc is not famed for its wines, although there are a few of note — St. Chinian, Minervois, Corbières and Roussillon. A good sparkling white, the Blanquet de Limoux, comes from the hills south of Carcassonne, and towards the Spanish border one of the specialities is the heavy, sweet port-like 'vin doux naturel' of Banyuls.

Fishing (above), is one of the main occupations of the people who live in the coastal areas of France where fish of every description are plentiful.

19

CHOOSING INGREDIENTS

The first rule about choosing ingredients is that you can't produce first-class results if the ingredients are second-class, and so in this section we have included information on the choosing and purchasing of main ingredients such as meat, fish, vegetables and fruit. These should always be the best quality you can afford, and they should be bought fresh and used as soon as possible. (Information on dry goods and other basic commodities is given in the section about the store cupboard.)

MEAT

Meat is one of the most expensive commodities any cook has to buy so it is important to know how to choose the best 'value for money'.

The flavour and tenderness of meat and game largely depends upon the time that it is allowed to hang. When an animal is killed, rigor mortis sets in which causes the muscles to contract. During the time the animal is allowed to hang thereafter, enzymes within the carcass start to work on the proteins in the meat, causing the muscle tissue to break down and become more tender. At the same time the flavour is released.

The hanging of meat will be done by the butcher, but because carcasses are bulky and hanging can take from seven to fourteen days, he is often tempted to sell the meat before it has thoroughly matured. When cut, meat that is well hung will darken quickly. If it has not been hung for long enough the bright orangey red colour will stay. Shoppers are often put off by this darker, less attractive colour, but they should not be because the quality will be much better. The fat on all meat should be a firm creamy colour and not at all sticky — stickiness denotes deterioration. Cuts of beef should be marbled with fat as this keeps the meat moist and tender. Pork and veal are not hung as they are killed while relatively young and therefore tender. When buying pork, look for pale pink fine-grained flesh with a small amount of white fat. There are two types of veal on the market: milk-fed, which has a mild flavour and the flesh of which is pale pink and delicate in texture; and barley-fed veal, which has a more pronounced flavour and is darker in colour.

It is a good thing to get to know your local butcher as he will be able to assist you in your choice of meat.

If you like to store meat in your deep freeze, there are a number of ways it can be purchased:

Pre-packed frozen cuts of meat, eg chops, stewing steak, chicken portions. Purchasing in this way, you are able to buy just the cuts you need, but only buy a reputable brand otherwise you may be disappointed with the quality which you cannot see when frozen.

Whole carcass sold either frozen or for you to freeze yourself. You may have a lot of wastage by purchasing in this way, and unless you are going to use all the different cuts of meat, it can be an expensive way of buying. Do be sure that the carcass will be butchered and if it is not frozen, do you have the facilities to freeze it properly?

A selection of cuts of meat of your choice in the quantity you require prepared and frozen by your local butcher. This is not the cheapest way of buying for your freezer but there is no wastage and you will be sure of the quality of the meat and the method of preparation.

When storing meat, poultry and game, cover loosely to allow the air to circulate and prevent the surface from drying out.

It is important to understand the method of cooking in your recipe so that if you cannot buy the exact cut required a substitution can be made. For example, any recipe using pheasant can equally well be made using chicken or guinea fowl.

FISH

There are many types of fresh fish available, most of which can be found all year round, although some are seasonal. Although the fish should be in season at a certain time of the year, supplies depend on the weather and the 'fisherman's catch', so may well vary from day to day. Your fishmonger can advise you which is the best 'value for money' but there are certain guidelines to the choosing of fresh fish which it is important to know:

♦ The flesh should be firm and springy. Soft watery flesh is a sign that the fish is stale.
♦ The eyes should be bright and not sunken.
♦ The gills should be red and moist.
♦ Where appropriate, the scales should be plentiful.
♦ The skin should have a fresh, moist, slimy appearance.
♦ There should be no unpleasant smell — it should smell of fish, not of ammonia.

If possible, buy fish on the day it is to be cooked. However, it may be stored in a refrigerator loosely covered for a short time.

Fish can be bought frozen, either whole or ready prepared, but only buy a reputable brand otherwise you may be disappointed with the quality which you cannot see when frozen. The flavour of fish deteriorates if kept for too long in the deep freeze and it must be well wrapped to prevent freezer burn.

It is useful to know how to clean and fillet fish at home because, although the fishmonger will do this for you, you will pay more per pound for ready-prepared fish.

There are three basic types of fish — white fish, oily fish and shellfish. Within the first category, the types of white fish used in recipes are interchangeable. Oily fish tend to have a more distinctive flavour, so be careful when substituting — do not use herring in place of trout. Any selection of shellfish can be mixed together according to taste, and in recipes calling for one type a substitution of your choice can be made.

Alternatively, fish can be bought smoked, either hot or cold. Hot smoking incorporates cooking, therefore the fish does not have to be re-cooked. This is the type of fish to use for cold pâtés, mousses or as an hors d'oeuvre; for example, smoked mackerel. Cold smoking does not heat

Dried herbs are a poor substitute for the taste and aroma of fresh ones. Apart from adding flavour to dishes, herbs can be used as a garnish, adding that 'finishing touch' to a well presented dish. As numbered: **1** parsley, a strong, fresh flavour which goes well with fish; **2** sage, a very pungent herb which should be used sparingly and is often used in stuffings; **3** marjoram, a sweet, spicy taste — good with green vegetables; **4** rosemary, a clean woody taste which is particularly good with lamb; **5** dill, slightly reminiscent of caraway seeds and goes well with salads; **6** mint, refreshing with yoghurt dressings and wonderful with new potatoes; **7** basil, although a member of the mint family it tastes more like cloves with a hint of liquorice and is especially good with vegetables; **8** thyme, a warm, pungent flavour which especially complements chicken and pork; **9** chives, a mild onion flavour suited to all types of dressings; **10** bay leaves, a bitter yet spicy flavour which works well with pasta; **11** fennel, a strong anise flavour which can substitute for parsley and is good with fish; **12** tarragon, a slightly anise flavour complementary to seafood and chicken, as well as being used to flavour French vinegar.

3

8

7

11

10

12

the fish which *must* be cooked before serving; for example, smoked haddock and kippers.

VEGETABLES

Most vegetables are seasonal. These days a great many are imported so it is possible to buy a good variety at all times of the year.

It is important to buy *fresh* vegetables, as the flavour and food value deteriorate with age. Leaf vegetables should not be limp and wilting and should have a strong colour. Root vegetables should be firm and dry — a withered appearance or moist mouldy patches are a bad sign. The size of vegetables is important: if they are too small the flavour will not have developed; if they are too large the texture may be coarse and tough.

A wide range of frozen vegetables is available, the quality of which varies. These can be useful, but fresh produce is always preferable.

Since the availability of good-quality produce depends a great deal on the weather, you may find that you have to make a substitution in a menu at the last minute. This need not cause too many problems if you choose a similar vegetable from the same family, for example, cauliflower and broccoli.

DAIRY PRODUCE

Cream There are three types of cream — single, whipping and double cream. Single cream can be used to enrich sauces, soups etc, as well as for pouring on desserts. Whipping cream has a lower fat content than double cream and so when whipped the result is lighter and the consistency softer. It can be used successfully in mousses and cold soufflés but without the gelatine that is present in both of these, the cream will eventually become watery. It cannot be whipped stiffly enough to pipe successfully. Double cream, because of its high fat content, needs careful handling. It should be well chilled before whisking or the result will be over-thick and heavy, and will curdle quickly.

In some recipes natural yoghurt can be substituted for half or all of the cream to give a lighter, fresher tasting result.

Commercially prepared soured cream is single cream with a special culture added to it. It cannot be made at home from pasteurized cream, but the addition of a little lemon juice to fresh cream will thicken it and give a mild acid taste. This can be used in place of soured cream.

Butter The two types of butter mainly used are salted and unsalted. Salted butter is used in pastries, cakes and for frying in a number of recipes. Unsalted butter is used for butter-creams and in puddings and desserts. It can also be used for frying and will not burn as quickly as salted butter, therefore is useful when residual pan juices are being made into a sauce. The flavour the butter imparts to the food is often essential for a good result so do not substitute unless absolutely necessary.

Eggs are graded according to size — size 1 being the largest and size 6 being the smallest. For the recipes in this book we have used size 3. The colour of the shell — brown or white — in no way affects the flavour or food value of the egg. Free-range or battery farmed eggs are available. Whichever you choose, freshness is important. Be sure to shop where the turnover is rapid.

FRUIT

Home-grown fruit is seasonal but with the addition of imported varieties, most fruits are available all year round.

When buying fruit it is better to buy produce that is on open display rather than pre-packed so that the fruit may be inspected for blemishes or bruises and tested for ripeness. If the fruit is to be used immediately, it should be purchased ripe, otherwise choose slightly unripe fruit and allow it to ripen at home. Ripe fruits should be stored in the refrigerator to prevent *over*-ripening, but fruits not quite ready to eat should be kept at room temperature.

Some fruits can be bought frozen, but the variety available is not large. Most fruits on the other hand are available in cans, but this process does alter the texture and sometimes the flavour of the fruit. Therefore, this type of fruit is only suitable for certain recipes. A number of fruits are dried which again alters the texture, appearance and flavour of the fruit, but when soaked and cooked some of these — particularly apricots — are a good substitute in a recipe.

In some recipes the type of fruit used can be varied as long as a similar fruit is used. For example, apples and pears are interchangeable, as are strawberries and raspberries, and prunes and apricots can be interchangeable.

THE STORE CUPBOARD

Stocking a store cupboard can be an expensive business so it is important to buy wisely. The amount and type of food kept in the store cupboard will largely depend upon: the space available; the time available for shopping; and the proximity to the shops. Main ingredients, such as meat, fish and vegetables, should always be bought and used fresh, but here we discuss the items which are necessary or useful for everyday eating and cooking, with hints on their storage.

Some items for the store cupboard can be bought in bulk but those items used in small amounts or infrequently must be purchased with thought to prevent wastage — curry powder and ground spices, for instance, should be bought and stored in small quantities only. Throughout the year there are various special offers available. Only take advantage of these if they are of use to you and not simply because they seem to be good value for money. Buy sensibly in quantities that can be used within the storage life of the food.

To complement the recipes in this book, we have suggested you keep the basic commodities listed overleaf, but they may be varied according to your own needs.

THE STORE CUPBOARD

The following items must be stored in airtight containers and kept in a dry atmosphere:

PLAIN FLOUR, STRONG FLOUR	Will keep for at least 6 months. Purchase brown flour only when required as it does not have a long shelf life.
CORNFLOUR, ARROWROOT	Store small amounts of each of these. They will keep for over 12 months.
CASTER SUGAR, GRANULATED SUGAR, SOFT BROWN SUGAR, ICING SUGAR	Will keep for over 12 months.
MIXED SPICE, CINNAMON ground and sticks, SAFFRON, WHOLE CLOVES, WHOLE NUTMEGS	Once opened the flavour of the spices will deteriorate. Use ground spices within 6 months and whole spices within 12 months.
CURRY POWDER	Only buy small amounts.
BLACK PEPPER, WHITE PEPPER, CAYENNE, PAPRIKA	Whole peppercorns retain their flavour for an indefinite period. Ground black and white pepper lose their flavour quickly. The red peppers may attract mites if kept for a long time.
SALT table and rock	Keeps well for up to 12 months.
BICARBONATE OF SODA CREAM OF TARTAR, BAKING POWDER	The strength of these deteriorates when they are opened. They will, therefore, only keep for up to 3 months.

The following items should be stored in a cool dry place:

TOMATO PUREE	An opened tube is usable for 6 months. A jar or can must be used within 48 hours of opening.
FRENCH MUSTARD Dijon, Tarragon etc	Keeps well for an indefinite period, but will dry out if stored incorrectly.
MALT/WINE VINEGAR white, red, tarragon	Will keep for an indefinite period if tightly sealed.
OIL corn, olive, vegetable, grape seed	Will keep for approximately 12 months.
WINE FOR COOKING white, red	Once opened it should be used within 48 hours.
SHERRY and CIDER	Once opened they should be used within 6 months.
BRANDY and KIRSCH	Will keep for an indefinite period if tightly sealed.
LEMON JUICE bottled	Once opened use within 6 months.
JAM, JELLY, HONEY, SYRUP	Once opened best used within 6 months.
VANILLA PODS	If rinsed and dried thoroughly after each use, they will keep well stored in an airtight container. Once the vanilla pod starts to lose its flavour, use it for vanilla sugar (see page 53).
VANILLA SUGAR	Store in an airtight container for up to 2 months.
LEAF GELATINE	This will keep indefinitely in an airtight container.
ALMONDS unblanched, blanched, flaked, ground	Use within 3 months
CURRANTS, SULTANAS, RAISINS ANGELICA, GLACE CHERRIES	Will keep for approximately 12 months.
GREEN FOOD COLOURING, CARMINE COLOURING	Will keep for an indefinite period.
INSTANT COFFEE	Once opened use as soon as possible.

PLAIN CHOCOLATE	Will keep for approximately 12 months.
HARICOT BEANS	Will keep for a indefinite period.
LONG-GRAIN RICE, PUDDING RICE	Will keep for an indefinite period.
YEAST	Buy fresh only when required and store in a refrigerator. Dried yeast keeps well for up to 6 months.
STOCK CUBES always better to make your own stock but in an emergency use them at half strength	Will keep for approximately 12 months.
CANNED TOMATOES	Will keep unopened for approximately 12 months. Once opened use immediately.
GARLIC	Fresh garlic will keep for about 1 month. A tube of garlic paste will keep for about 3 months. Garlic powder or granules will keep for approximately 12 months.

The following frozen items are a useful addition to the store cupboard:

BREAD white and brown	Will keep for approximately 4 weeks. A cut loaf will defrost quickly for croûtons. Ready made breadcrumbs freeze well.
CREAM double and whipping	Freeze in small amounts when you have a surplus.
CREAM	Buy commercially frozen.
FRESH YEAST	Freeze in 15g/½oz quantities. Keeps for approximately 4 weeks. Once defrosted the yeast becomes liquid but is perfectly satisfactory for use.
SOFT FRUITS	Strawberries, raspberries and blackcurrants are useful for purées and desserts.
VEGETABLES	French beans, peas, asparagus and broccoli are useful for garnishing.

The following items, to be stored in a refrigerator, are a useful addition to the store cupboard and should be purchased regularly:

BUTTER LARD, DRIPPING	Unsalted butter deteriorates quickly and should only be purchased when required.
CHEESE	Should be covered with cling film to prevent drying out. Good quality Cheddar can be used in all recipes. Only buy other varieties when required.
MILK	It is always useful to keep a carton of ultra heat treated (UHT) milk in the store cupboard for emergencies.
BACON back and streaky	Should be covered with cling film to prevent drying out.
ORANGES and LEMONS	These keep well in the bottom compartment and are useful for flavouring and garnishing.
PARSLEY	Keep washed in a polythene bag.
CARROTS and CELERY	These keep crisp in the bottom compartment.

The following perishable items should be stored in a cool place and should be purchased regularly:

EGGS	These should always be at room temperature when used for cooking. (If eggs are stored in a refrigerator allow them to return to room temperature before using.)
POTATOES	These should be stored in a dark airy place.
ONIONS	Store separately to prevent cross contamination.
FRESH HERBS	Store in a jug of water.

COOKING METHODS

Food is cooked for a variety of reasons, the most important being to kill bacteria or parasites that may be in the food (for example, salmonella inside raw chicken). Because cooking destroys bacteria it will also prolong the keeping time a little. Cooking food makes it more digestible as some food cannot be assimilated by the body in its raw state (for example, raw potatoes are highly indigestible). Cooking also tenderizes food, especially meat, making it easier to masticate and, therefore, digest. Cooking makes food more palatable and often improves its appearance (for example, red haemoglobin in meat changes to brown). It also develops the flavour of some food, and the smell of food cooking will stimulate the digestive juices. Cooking food allows some hot and some cold dishes to be incorporated in a menu, also giving a variety of textures.

BOILING

Boiling is a means of cooking food in liquid at 212°F/100°C. Some foods such as vegetables, rice, pasta, etc. are boiled for the whole of the cooking time because a reduction of temperature would cause softening of the outer crust and the water would be absorbed by the food. Other foods such as meat, dumplings, etc. are boiled for the first ten minutes. This preliminary high temperature causes the coagulation of protein or the starch grains to burst on the outside of the food. The heat is then lowered, otherwise the protein would become tough or the starchy food would break up.

SIMMERING

Simmering is cooking in liquid at 190°F/88°C. In most cases the liquid is brought to boiling point and then reduced to simmering when bubbles should rise gently on one side of the pan. It is important to know the difference between boiling and simmering as food that needs to be simmered will be ruined by continuous boiling and vice versa.

POACHING

Food is generally only half covered with liquid when cooking by this method. The temperature should be just below that of simmering, with the liquid barely moving. This is a very gentle method of cooking suitable for delicate fish, fruit, etc. For ease of turning the food over, poaching is generally carried out in a shallow pan.

STEWING

Stewing is a slow method of cooking using a moist heat. It differs from boiling in that a comparatively small amount of liquid is used. It may either be carried out in a casserole in a low oven or on the top of the stove. This method of cooking will tenderize tough cuts of meat — although they should be lean otherwise the finished result will be greasy — and it is also suitable for dried fruits such as prunes, apricots, etc.

BRAISING

Sometimes referred to as 'pot-roasting', braising is cooking meat, poultry, fish or vegetables on a bed of diced vegetables — known as a 'mirepoix' — in a strong pan with a well-fitting lid. The liquid should just cover the mirepoix. There should be sufficient space left around the food so that it does not touch the dish and therefore become scorched.

STEAMING

This is a very slow method of cooking, but there is very little risk of overcooking the food and making it indigestible. The process may be carried out either in a steamer over a pan of boiling water — the steamer must have a tight-fitting lid — or in a basin standing in the boiling water. The basin is usually placed on an upturned saucer or a cutter to prevent the base becoming too hot. The saucepan must have a well-fitting lid. Regular replenishing of the boiling water is essential for both methods.

GRILLING

Grilling is a fast method of cooking by dry heat. It is only suitable for small tender cuts of meat or fish. Food cooked in this way does not become greasy and is therefore easily digested. This method of cooking may be carried out over a hot fire or under a red hot gas or electric grill.

BAKING/ROASTING

Baking is a dry form of cooking carried out in an enclosed oven. Roasting is a term particularly applied to the cooking of meat in front of a clear open fire, but because of the construction of modern cookers, baking has now replaced roasting and a joint cooked in the oven is described as 'roast'. Potatoes and other vegetables basted with fat and cooked around the meat are referred to as 'roast' whereas a scrubbed potato in its skin is referred to as 'baked'.

FRYING

There are three types of frying, each suitable for different varieties of food — dry, shallow and deep fat. For all types of frying it is important to use clean fat or oil and have the correct degree of heat. If the fat is too cool it will be absorbed by the food which will then become sodden and greasy. If the fat is too hot the outside of the food will become black and charred before the inside of the food is cooked. Only fry small quantities of food, as the addition of cold food to hot fat will reduce the temperature of the fat or oil. Some delicately textured food needs protection from the heat of the fat to allow the food to cook through without burning. Therefore, it may be coated with seasoned flour, egg and breadcrumbs or batter. This particularly applies to food which is to be deep fried. All fried food must be drained well on absorbent paper before serving. If fried food needs to be kept warm for a short period of time, it must be left uncovered or the steam will cause the food to become soggy.

PREPARATIONS AND TECHNIQUES

Many of the preparations and techniques illustrated here crop up time and again in the recipe sections. We hope that they will clarify the trickier aspects of the more complicated recipes in this book, and provide useful reference.

MAKING PATE FEUILLETEE (PUFF PASTRY)

The flavour obtained by making your own Pâte Feuilletée (Puff Pastry) using butter is well worth the time and effort involved. The process is very repetitious so only the most important steps have been shown here. (A detailed recipe is given on page 70.)

1 Sift the flour and salt onto a board and make a well in the centre approximately 15cm/6 inches in diameter. Pour in half the water and work all the ingredients with your fingertips.

2 The mixture is ready when it resembles Sauce Béchamel and does not flow together when a finger is drawn through it.

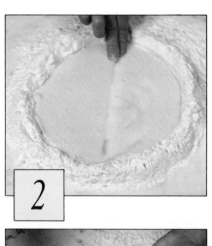

3 Using the fingertips of both hands, palms upwards, flake the dry flour through the mixture in the centre.

4 Repeat this from all sides of the well until the pastry is dry and flaky. Sprinkle half the remaining water over the dough and flake again.

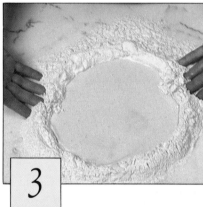

5 Gradually add the remaining water to the dough and roll into a ball.

6 Knead lightly and wrap the pastry in a polythene bag or cling film. Allow to chill. The dough is now known as a 'détrempe'.

7 Lightly flour the work surface and roll the détrempe into a circle approximately 25cm/10 inches in diameter.

8 Soften the butter by tapping it with a rolling pin to elongate it. Cut in half, reform and repeat until the butter measures 10×15cm/4×6 inches.

9 Place the butter in the middle of the dough and fold the dough over from the right and left to cover the butter, leaving a border of 2.5cm/1 inch.

10 Press the dough lightly with a rolling pin to elongate it.

11 Fold the bottom third of the dough up to cover the middle third.

12 Fold the top third down — the dough is now known as a 'pâton'.

13 Seal the edges gently, give the dough a quarter turn, and roll to a rectangle approximately 18×38cm/ 7×15 inches. Repeat the folds exactly as described above. It should have 6 rollings and foldings in all.

In this picture (right), a selection of French cooking pots and equipment which is available in most good kitchen shops is shown. Top left clockwise: **1** 9½pt round cocotte; **2** 5¾pt round cocotte; **3** 3¾pt round cocotte; **4** 4½pt oval casserole; **5** stainless steel vegetable mill; **6** 3pt oval casserole; **7** steel crêpe pan.

Making PATE BRISEE

As with many French pastries, Pâte Brisée is quick and easy to make on a board. The finished ball of dough must not be at all crumbly before chilling ready for use. When lined into a flan ring, the pastry case may be 'baked blind' or baked with a filling.

1 Sift the dry ingredients onto a board and make a well in the centre. Add the slightly softened pieces of butter together with the egg.

2 Rub all the ingredients with the fingertips, breaking up the butter and egg with the flour.

3 Continue rubbing all the ingredients together, and form into a smooth ball of pliable dough.

LINING A FLAN RING

1 Roll the pastry to a circle approximately 5cm/2 inches larger than the flan ring. Lift the pastry on the rolling pin and place it in the ring.

2 Using the fingertips push the pastry firmly against the flan ring, making sure that no air is trapped beneath the pastry and baking sheet.

3 Fold the excess pastry to the outside of the flan ring and form a lip of pastry around the top. Roll off the excess.

4 Carefully lift the lip so that it stands up above the flan ring. Make sure that there is no pastry overhanging.

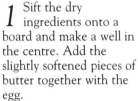

33

Making Croissants

Croissants can be frozen very successfully either before or after cooking — there is no more effort involved in making two or three times the recipe and freezing some. You must allow yourself the pleasure of one straight from the oven as a reward for your time and effort.

1 Sift the dry ingredients onto the work surface and make a large well in the centre. Put in the yeast and 2 tablespoons of the water.

2 Using your fingertips, mix the yeast and water together.

3 Gradually add the remaining water and continue mixing it in with your fingertips.

4 With your fingertips, gradually draw the flour from the sides into the centre of the well.

5 Bring the dough together into a soft ball. Cover the ball of dough until it has doubled in size, and allow to chill for 2-3 hours or overnight.

6 Sprinkle a little flour onto the work surface to prevent the dough sticking. Roll the dough in to a circle about 25cm/ 10 inches in diameter.

7 Soften the butter by tapping it with a rolling pin to elongate it, cut in half, reform and repeat until the butter measures 10×15cm/4×6 inches.

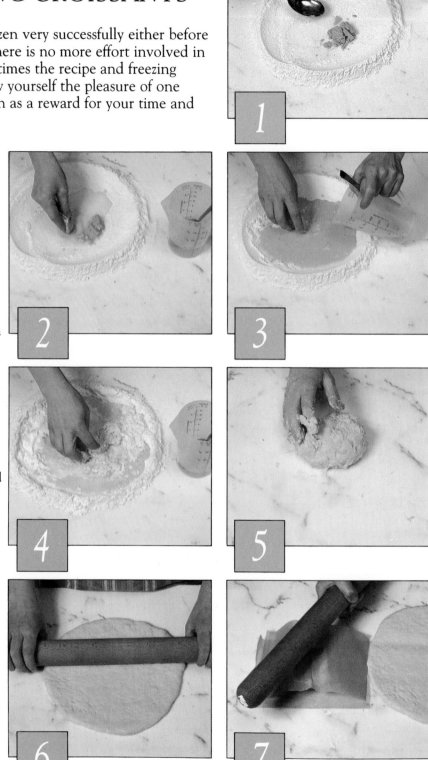

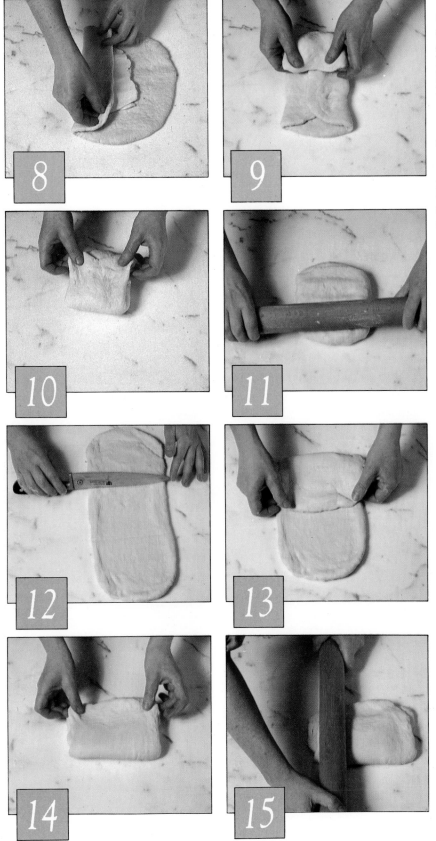

8 Place the butter in the middle of the dough and fold over the dough from the right and left to cover the butter, leaving a border of 2.5cm/ 1 inch.

9 Fold the bottom third up to cover the middle third.

10 Bring the top third down to keep the layers uniform, and the butter from squeezing out.

11 Complete the sealing process by pressing the joins lightly with a rolling pin from top to bottom.

12 Roll the dough into a rectangle approximately 36×18cm/ 14×7 inches and mark lightly into three.

13 Fold the bottom third of the rectangle of dough up to cover the middle third.

14 Bring the top third down to keep the layers uniform and seal the edges.

15 Complete the sealing process by pressing the edges lightly with a rolling pin from side to side.

35

16 Give the dough a quarter turn and repeat the rolling and folding 4 times in all. Chill well before rolling it out for use.

17 Roll the dough to a rectangle 20×56cm/8×22 inches and trim 5mm/¼ inch from each edge. Cut into 5 triangles and form the sixth triangle from the 2 end pieces of the dough.

18 Place a thin strip of the trimming along the base of each triangle.

19 Fold the base of the triangle over the strip of the trimming, pressing lightly with your fingertips.

20 Using the fingertips, start to roll towards the point of the triangle.

21 Continue rolling with the palm of the hand until the point is reached.

22 Stop rolling when the tip of the triangle is underneath.

23 Form into a horseshoe shape and keep in a warm place until double in size. Brush with beaten egg and bake for about 15 minutes at 230°C/450°F/Gas Mark 8.

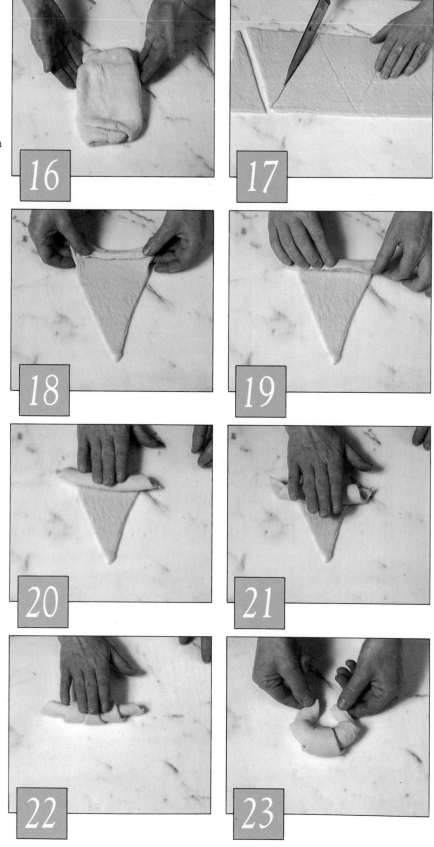

MAKING BOUCHEES

There are numerous fillings that can be used for bouchées, which may be served hot or cold. Any excess pastry can be re-rolled to make cheese straws, sausage rolls or sweet biscuits.

1 Roll out the Pâte Feuilletée (see p. 30) to a 33cm/13 inch square and cut out 16 circles 7.5cm/3 inches in diameter.

2 With both hands, carefully remove the excess pastry without spoiling the shape of the circle. Keep chilled.

3 Brush lightly with beaten egg.

4 Mark each circle with a lattice pattern using the back of a knife

5 Using a 4.5cm/1¾ inch cutter, press down firmly and remove the centres from 8 circles.

6 Carefully put a circle with its centre removed on each whole circle and press down firmly. Chill before baking for 15-20 minutes at 230°C/450°F/Gas Mark 8.

7 With the point of a knife, remove the round of pastry that rises to the centre and keep for a lid. Scoop out any uncooked pastry from inside each bouchée with a teaspoon. Return the bouchées to a cooler oven for 5-7 minutes to dry out, at 190°C/375°F/Gas Mark 5.

CLEANING AND FILLETING TROUT

When serving trout for a main course, choose fish weighing 275-350g/10-12oz. If it is to be served as a first course, a fish of approximately 225g/8oz is large enough.

1 Place the trout flat on a board, using kitchen scissors to remove the fins. Trim the tail, keeping the original shape.

2 Make a slit along the belly and gut the fish. Remove the clot of blood which lies along the backbone with the tip of the knife.

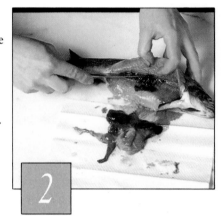

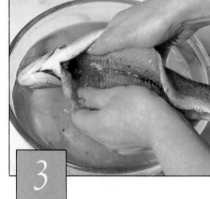

3 Open the fish and wash the body cavity in a bowl of water. Dry with kitchen paper.

4 Place the fish on its belly cavity and press it firmly along the backbone.

5 Turn the fish over and cut through the backbone close to the tail and the head.

6 Carefully remove the backbone from the flesh. Remove any loose bones that are left in the fish.

7 Fold the fish back into shape and remove the eyes, using your thumbnail or the point of a knife.

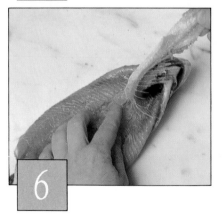

SKINNING AND FILLETING SOLE

Many types of flat fish are filleted in the same way as lemon sole. A little salt on the fingertips will stop the fish slipping as you carry out this process.

The skin of Dover sole is easier to remove before filleting. The fish is often served whole and filleted at the table.

LEMON SOLE

1 Make an incision around the head and down the backbone, then mark the skin between the fillets and fins on either side.

2 Remove the fillets by cutting through the flesh at the top of the backbone, allowing the knife to scrape along the bones from head to tail.

3 With the fillet skin side down, hold the tail firmly and work towards the head, at the same time pulling the fillet towards you.

DOVER SOLE

1 Place the fish with its dark skin facing upwards. Then remove all the fins with scissors.

2 Make an incision in the skin just above the tail and loosen the skin with the thumbnail, working around each side of the fish to the head.

3 Hold the tail firmly with one hand and pull the skin away sharply. The white skin is removed in the same way.

4 Remove the fillets as in step 2 for lemon sole (above).

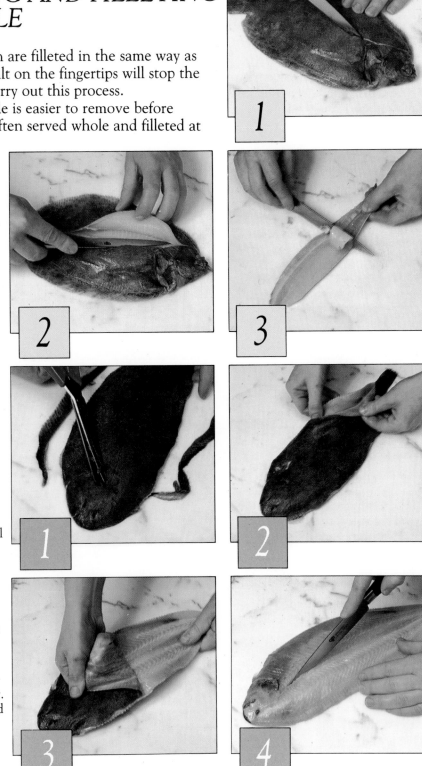

PREPARING LOBSTER

The flavour and texture of frozen lobster cannot be compared to the succulence of a really fresh lobster plainly cooked. They are easy to prepare and have very few inedible parts. The intestine is not always visible; if the lobster has been starved the thin black line which runs through the meat near the tail is not present.

1 Place the lobster on a board with the tail spread out flat and push the point of a cook's knife firmly into the cross on top of the head.

2 Hold the side of the lobster firmly and bring the knife down to where the tail meets the head, splitting it in two.

3 Remove the sac behind the eyes and, if it is visible, the intestine vein in the meat near the tail.

4 Gently insert the sharp end of a knife into the tail, and with a backwards and forwards movement remove the flesh.

5 Holding half of the lobster firmly on the board, pull off the claws.

6 Discard the 'dead men's fingers'. These can be found beneath the shell with the small claws attached.

7 Crack the claws with a heavy weight and remove the white flesh with a skewer. Prepare the other half of the lobster in the same way.

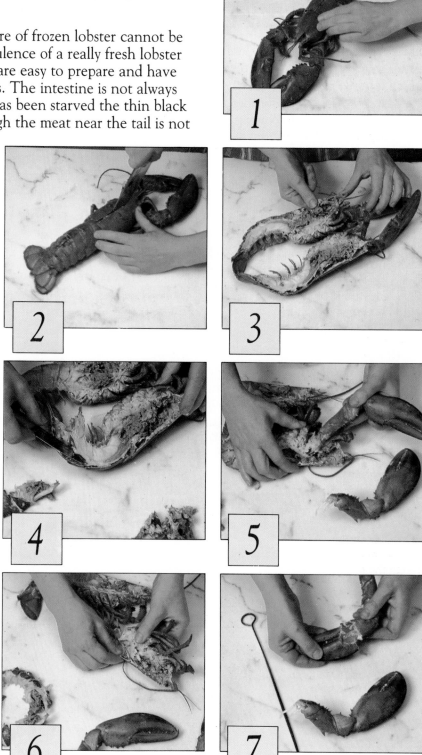

PREPARING CRAB

Care must be taken when removing the flesh from the crab that no pieces of shell are included. The white and brown meat are sometimes mixed together, but often kept separate and put back in the shell.

1 Holding the crab firmly with one hand, remove the claws and pincers with the other hand. Then open the crab by pressing on the body.

2 Pull the body away from the shell and discard the 'dead men's fingers' from around the body.

3 Holding the shell in one hand, remove the stomach sac, which is found behind the eyes.

4 Remove the brown meat from the shell.

5 Crack the pincers with a heavy weight and use a skewer to extract the white meat from them.

6 Break the small claws and remove any meat from the largest section with a skewer. Then cut through the body and remove the white meat.

7 Press firmly on the shell around the natural marked line to neaten the shape. Scrub the shell well before replacing the flesh.

There is a wide range of equipment available to aid the cook in every specialized area of cookery, but a good set of knives is an essential part of every cook's kitchen.

From top left as numbered: **1** double cherry stoner; **2** Parisienne cutter or melon baller; **3** bell cutter; **4** star cutter; **5** bird cutter; **6** half moon cutter; **7** pig cutter; **8** ice cream cone cutter; **9** butterfly cutter; **10** set of fluted diamond cutters; **11** set of heart cutters; **12** fluted doughnut cutter; **13** plain doughnut cutter; **14** set of icing bags; **15** set of plain, fluted and special icing nozzles; **16** set of plain and fluted round cutters; **17** set of oval fluted cutters; **18** set of aspic cutters; **19** stainless steel ham slicer; **20** stainless steel salmon knife; **21** stainless steel 8 inch cook's knife; **22** stainless steel carver; **23** stainless steel 4 inch cook's knife; **24** curved trussing needle; **25** larding needle.

19

20

21

22

23

24

25

18

16

17

15

14

13

12

43

BONING A CHICKEN

This method of boning poultry or game produces a very well shaped finished product since it does not involve splitting the bird down the back. A large bird such as a turkey may be stuffed with a selection of smaller ones; for example a chicken or pheasant.

1 Lay the chicken on the work surface. Starting at the neck of the bird, scrape away the flesh to expose the wishbone.

2 Remove the wishbone with the fingertips. Scrape away the flesh from the rib cage until the wing joint is reached.

3 Scrape away the flesh from the wingbone up to the first joint, and cut through the joint between the carcass and wingbone.

4 To remove the wing hold the bird firmly on the work surface and remove the exposed bone by breaking the joint. Repeat with the other wing.

5 Holding the bird in the same position, continue scraping down the rib cage.

6 Lay the chicken on its breast and gently pull the skin back when scraping along the underside of the keel in order not to puncture the skin.

7 Continue scraping down the carcass until the leg joint is reached. Then push the leg through so that it is exposed.

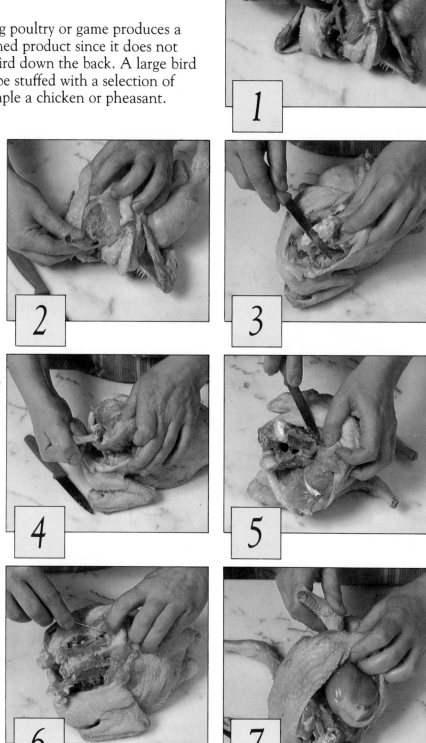

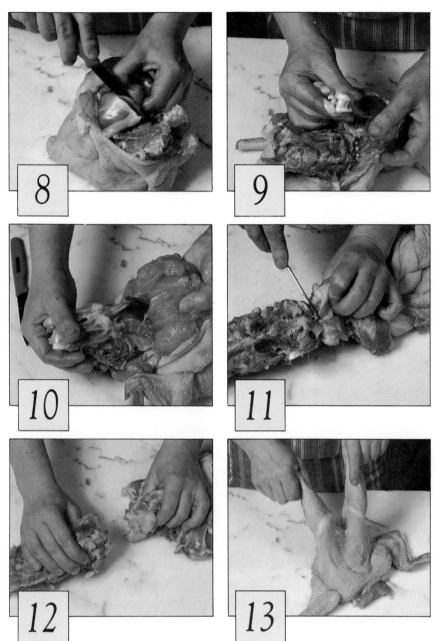

8 Holding the leg with one hand, cut through the joint of the drumstick.

9 Cut away the flesh from the thigh joint and remove the bone. Leave the drumstick in place. Repeat at other side.

10 Continue scraping the flesh from the carcass, turning back the flesh as you proceed. Take great care when removing the flesh from the ridge of the breast bone.

11 When the rib cage is completely exposed, cut through the membrane, then carefully work down the carcass to the parson's nose and cut through.

12 The parson's nose may either be left with the flesh (as shown) or attached to the keel and used for stock.

13 Hold the drumsticks firmly and shake the bird back into shape. Stuff and truss as required.

JOINTING A CHICKEN

There are various ways of jointing poultry. This method is particularly simple and gives eight joints of similar size and appearance. Depending on the size of the chicken, you may serve one or two joints per person. The keel may be used to make stock.

1 Lay the chicken on a board. Hold the leg firmly and cut through the skin so the inside leg joint is exposed.

2 Pull the leg away from the bird to break the ball and socket joint. Cut through the flesh as close to the carcass as you can. Repeat with the other leg.

3 Divide the thigh and the drumstick by cutting through the centre ball and socket joint.

4 Place the drumstick on the board and with a sharp knife remove the end of the drumstick. Repeat with the other drumstick.

5 Pinch the white breast meat above the wing joint. Remove the flesh with the wing joint by cutting the joint as close as you can to the carcass.

6 Remove the wing tip and fold the joint into a neat shape with the attached breast meat over the wingbone.

7 Smooth the skin over the joint to neaten it and hold it in place.

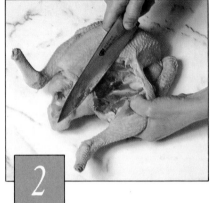

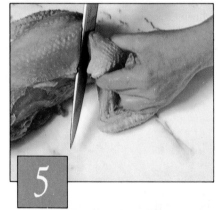

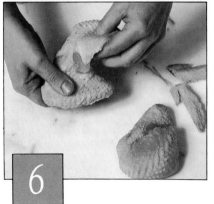

8 To remove the whole breast, first separate the keel by cutting through the rib cage along the side of the body.

9 Cut through the breast bone at an angle to divide the breast into 2 joints of equal size.

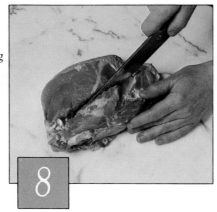
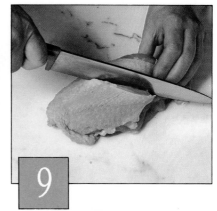

Trussing a Chicken

1 Insert a trussing needle threaded with string through the leg at the joint. Push the needle through the carcass so that it emerges in the corresponding place on the other side.

2 Leaving a gap of approximately 6cm/2½ inches, insert the needle through the flesh of the leg, through the carcass and out the other side.

3 Remove the needle, pull the strings together to make a neat shape and tie in position.

4 Fold the wings neatly against the side of the bird. Insert a trussing needle threaded with string between the two bones of the wing joint and push the needle through the carcass so that it emerges in the corresponding place on the other side. Leaving a gap of approximately 5cm/2 inches, insert the needle through the wing, through the carcass and out the other side.

5 Remove the trussing needle. Pull the strings together to make a neat shape.

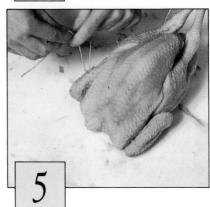
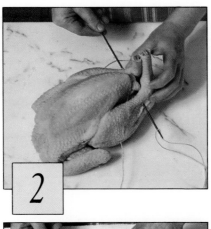
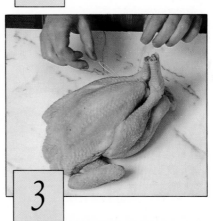
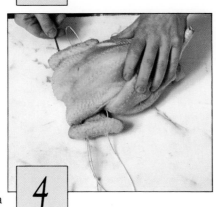

PREPARING GLOBE ARTICHOKES

Artichoke bottoms make an interesting garnish. The preparation of them may seem wasteful, but only the very base of the leaves is edible.

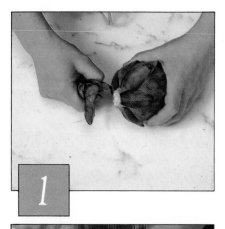

1 Hold the artichoke firmly in both hands and break off the stalk.

2 Using a sharp knife, cut the leaves all round the base, trimming as closely as possible until only the neatly shaped heart is left.

3 Hold the bottom of the artichoke firmly and cut the centre core of the leaves just above the heart.

4 Here is the 'choke' in the centre of the vegetable before it has been cooked. Squeeze over a little lemon juice to prevent discoloration.

5 After the artichoke has been cooked in boiling salted water for about 20-30 minutes, drain and refresh. Then pull out the leaves to expose the 'choke'.

6 With a teaspoon, carefully remove the hairy 'choke', taking care not to damage the bottom.

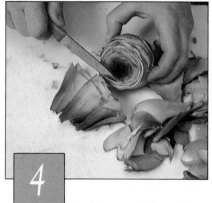

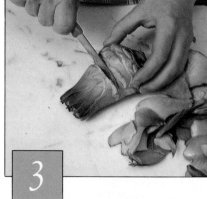

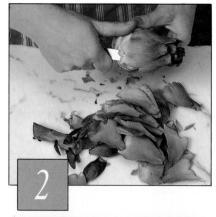

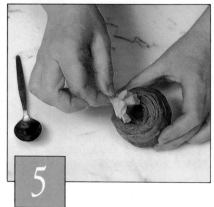

There are specific dishes for every kind of recipe (left). Here we show a selection which can be adapted to other uses. **1** Madeleine sheet; **2** 10 inch plain flan ring; **3** cream horn moulds; **4** oval pie mould; **5** plain flan/sandwich tin; **6** charlotte mould; **7** savarin mould: closed tube.

Certain dishes have to be served directly from the vessels in which they were cooked or prepared (right), so it is a good idea to have a selection of kitchenware which does not spoil the look of the finally set dinner table. **1** 3½pt porcelain soufflé dish; **2** 1½pt porcelain soufflé dish; **3** 9½oz porcelain soufflé dish; **4** earthenware kugelhopf; **5** 4oz porcelain Coeur à Creme dishes.

USEFUL TIPS

The following are selected explanations and classifications of cookery techniques which are referred to time and again throughout the book. For cookery terms, see p. 216.

STOCKS, MARINADES AND SAUCES

◆ Stocks must be made with good quality ingredients and prepared well in advance so that excess fat may be skimmed from them. It is always preferable to make your own stock. Stock cubes can be used in an emergency but be careful as they tend to be salty and strong.

◆ Marinating meat, game or fish helps to tenderize and improve the flavour. As the liquid is often used in the finished dish, it is important that the flavourings complement the main ingredients.

◆ Foundation sauces form a major part of a number of recipes. These must be made with care as the flavour and appearance of the finished dish can be spoilt.

FISH AND SHELLFISH

◆ Live lobsters are bluish black in colour and when cooked they turn bright red. They should be cooked in boiling salted water for 15 minutes for the first 450g/1lb and then 10 minutes for each further 450g/1lb. Drain well and allow to cool before using.

◆ Crabs are cooked in exactly the same way.

MEAT AND POULTRY

◆ To make the carving of poultry easier, remove the wishbone before cooking (see illustrations of boning a chicken on p. 44).

◆ To flatten veal escalopes, place between two sheets of cling film or non-stick silicone paper—do not use greaseproof paper as the escalopes will stick to it—and beat with a rolling pin or meat mallet to flatten.

VEGETABLES AND HERBS

♦ To crush a clove of garlic, first remove the papery skin. Chop finely, sprinkle with a good pinch of salt and crush to a paste with the blade of a knife. If the garlic does not form a paste easily, a little more salt can be added. Garlic prepared in this way blends easily into any moist mixture without leaving unpleasant lumps in the food.

♦ To chop parsley finely, first wash it and dry well. Remove the stalks and chop the leafy part very finely with a large cook's knife. The parsley can then be placed in a small square of muslin or the corner of a clean tea towel, washed again and squeezed out thoroughly before use. This will give a very fine dry brightly coloured result.

♦ To prepare red or green peppers, cut in half, remove the pith and seeds and discard them. Rinse the pepper under cold running water to remove any remaining seeds and use the pepper as required.

♦ Remove the stalk end from a tomato with the point of a knife. Cover with boiling water and leave for 10 seconds. Remove and place in cold water and the skin can then be easily removed.

FRUIT

♦ To segment an orange, cut a slice from the top and bottom. Stand the fruit on one of the cut ends and cut away the skin and pith until all the flesh is exposed. Hold the fruit at the top and bottom and cut between the membrane with a sharp knife to remove each segment, folding back each membrane as you go.

♦ To make a purée from canned or poached fruit, drain the fruit and blend in the liquidizer or food processor, adding a little of the fruit syrup if the mixture is too thick. Sieve and use as required.

PASTRY

♦ To knock up the edges of a savoury pie, hold the pastry with a floured finger and tap the edges with the back of a knife.

♦ To flute the edges for decoration, hold the pastry lightly with the thumb and draw the back of a knife across the knocked up edge at 2.5cm/1 inch intervals.

♦ To make leaves from pastry, cut a strip of pastry about 2.5cm/1 inch wide and cut into diamond shapes and mark veins with the back of a knife. Twist slightly to make a leaf.

BASIC SAVOURY PREPARATIONS

♦ When using breadcrumbs to coat food before frying, they should be sieved to give a neat and fine finish. If they are being used to sprinkle on the top of a dish to be served 'au gratin', bread can be made into crumbs in the liquidizer or food processor, and does not need to be sieved.

♦ When making croûtons or croûtes (which are slightly larger), use slightly stale bread. They should be approximately 1.25cm/½ inch thick and cut to the required size and shape. Fry in equal quantities of very hot butter and oil until golden brown. Drain well on kitchen paper before use. All croûtons used in this book should be prepared in this way.

BASIC SWEET PREPARATIONS

♦ There are two ways of browning flaked almonds. They may either be grilled for a very short time turning frequently, or they can be placed on a baking sheet in a hot oven for about 15-20 minutes or until golden brown.

♦ To make apricot glaze, warm a jar of apricot jam — a cheaper brand without whole fruit is best — then pass through a sieve into a clean pan.

Warm gently just before use. If it is a little thick add 1 teaspoon of lemon juice or water. Use while warm.

♦ In this book we have chosen to use leaf gelatine. This can be used in any recipe in the same proportion as powdered gelatine. Before use, leaf gelatine should be covered with cold water and soaked for 10-15 minutes then squeezed out thoroughly before dissolving in the hot liquid. If leaf gelatine is not available, the powdered variety may be substituted. This needs soaking in 3-4 tablespoons of cold liquid then warming gently over a pan of hot water, stirring all the time until dissolved. It can then be used as required.

GENERAL PREPARATIONS

♦ To prepare cake tins for baking, brush lightly with melted lard or oil. Never use butter or margarine as the high water and salt content of these will make the mixture stick and burn.

♦ To keep crêpes warm as they are cooking, cover a pan of hot water with a metal plate with an up-turned saucer on it. Lay each crêpe over this and cover the whole thing with a large bowl.

♦ There are various stages to look for when whisking egg whites. If they are to be used to lighten a mousse or soufflé, they should be whisked until they form stiff frothy peaks. If they are whisked until they look dry it will be difficult to fold them into the mixture. For meringues, the white should be whisked until they look dry, and stiff sharp peaks are formed.

♦ In all recipes in this book amounts of fat for greasing or dry goods for dusting are not included in the ingredients but are an extra.

♦ When greaseproof paper is used to keep steam from escaping from a saucepan, it must be tucked well down inside the pan so that it touches the food. In this way the moisture will stay in the pan.

♦ To use a Parisienne/vegetable ball cutter, press straight into the food until a half circle is made and the food is visible in the small hole in the cutter, then twist carefully in each direction and scoop out completely.

♦ To speed up the setting of gelatine-based mixtures, place the mixture in a mixing bowl (stainless steel will make the process even quicker). Stand this bowl in a large container of ice and cold water. The gelatine mixture must be stirred very frequently to prevent uneven setting. As soon as the mixture becomes jelly like, remove the bowl from the ice and water and use at once.

♦ To make vanilla sugar, grind one vanilla pod with 450g/1lb of granulated or caster sugar in a liquidizer or food processor, pass through a sieve, store in an airtight container and use as required. This will give you a concentrated vanilla sugar which may be used in place of vanilla essence.

♦ For any mixture that is whisked over hot water, bring a saucepan of water to the boil, remove from the heat and place the bowl over the hot water. The base of the bowl should not come into contact with the water as overheating will occur, just as it will if the saucepan is kept on the heat.

Menu Planning

When planning a menu, skill is needed to produce a meal which will combine a well-balanced diet with a pleasing colour scheme and variety of texture and flavour, and that can be cooked and served in the time allotted, with the equipment available. On many occasions, you will want to be both the cook and the hostess, and if you are to be successful in this role, the menu must be carefully planned so you do not have to spend too long in the kitchen after your guests arrive.

There are a few basic rules to give guidance when compiling a menu, and these are as follows:

♦ Consider the number of guests and the occasion for which the menu is required.

♦ The amount of time you have available to prepare and cook the meal is important. Do as much preparation as possible in advance, rather then leaving it all until just before your guests arrive.

♦ Be sure to plan a menu that does not require more top of stove cooking than you can cope with at any one time, or that requires two different oven temperatures at the same time, or more refrigerator space than you have available. With insufficient forethought, these minor irritations become major problems.

♦ If you do not know your guests' tastes, avoid very unusual or highly spiced foods. Shellfish can also be a difficult choice as a great many people find it unacceptable. Remember that some nationalities and religions prohibit the use of certain ingredients.

♦ Seasonal foods are not only the best 'value for money', but will be full of flavour and of top quality.

♦ Choose dishes that complement the season. For example, cool refreshing salads that would be welcome in the summer months are not as satisfying in the winter.

♦ Variety in the methods of cooking is important. Avoid for example, a series of foods served with a sauce.

♦ All dishes should be of a similar standard. Avoid over-elaboration in one course and extreme homeliness in another.

♦ Provide a pleasant variety in the colour and texture of the dishes so that they contrast with, yet complement, one another.

♦ Do not repeat any main ingredient in a later course. It would be wrong to follow celery soup with braised celery as a vegetable.

These are not in any order of importance but merely suggestions to help you compile your menus. Do remember, though, that it is no good planning a superb menu if you do not have the skill to carry it through. You should not be too adventurous when cooking for an important occasion — play safe and try the dishes out on the family first.

If you own a deep freeze and if time allows, some dishes can be prepared in advance and frozen until required. This relieves the pressure nearer the time.

If you own a microwave cooker, last-minute cooking of vegetables need not be a problem as they can be successfully re-heated in their serving dishes having been cooked conventionally earlier in the day.

When garnishing and decorating food, choose something that will both contrast with and complement the colour and texture of the food. Do not disguise the food completely. If possible, choose a garnish or decoration that gives some indication of the contents of the dish.

BAD MENU	REASONS WHY	IMPROVED MENU
MAQUEREAUX QUIMPER RAIE AU BEURRE NOIR POMMES DE TERRE DIJONNAISE MARQUISE ALICE	Repetition of fish in first and second course; butter and cream featuring heavily in all courses; repetition of mustard in first course and vegetable; chopped herbs featuring heavily throughout; very rich menu.	MAQUEREAUX QUIMPER ROTI DE PORC A L'AIL POMMES DE TERRE PARISIENNE CAROTTES A LA VICHY POIRES BELLE DIJONNAISE
PIPERADE BASQUAISE COTES DE PORC AUX PRUNEAUX RATATOUILLE A LA NICOISE TURBAN D'AGEN	Repetition of main ingredients in first course and vegetable and also in main course and dessert; soft texture throughout; very strong flavourings.	OEUFS TONNELIER BLANQUETTE D'AGNEAU DES BORDS DU RHONE GRATIN DAUPHINOISE TURBAN D'AGEN
GNOCCHI A LA PARISIENNE BOUCHEES A LA REINE SALADE DE FONDS D'ARTICHAUTS AUX CHAMPIGNONS SAVARIN	Repetition of pastry and sauce in first and second course; repetition of mushrooms in main course and salad; all dishes of a similar colour; very heavy texture and no variety of shape.	CONSOMME JULIENNE BOUCHEES A LA REINE SALADE AUX NOIX BAVAROIS RUBANE

SIZE OF AVERAGE PORTIONS PER PERSON (UNCOOKED WEIGHT)

SOUP	200-300ml/7-10fl oz
HORS D'OEUVRE	100g/4oz
FISH	off the bone 100g/4oz
FISH	on the bone 175g/6oz
WHOLE FISH	for a first course 225g/8oz for a main course 275-350g/10-12oz
MEAT	off the bone 100g/4oz on the bone 175g/6oz
CHEESE	50g/2oz
VEGETABLES	100g/4oz (more if there is a lot of wastage)
GRAVY/SAVOURY SAUCE	25ml/1fl oz
COLD DESSERTS	100-175g/4-6oz
FRUIT	100g/4oz
PASTRY DESSERTS/CAKES	40g/1½oz flour (in basic mixture)
SWEET SAUCES	50ml/2fl oz
BEVERAGES	200ml/7fl oz

READING A RECIPE

Having decided that you will cook a particular dish, the end result will be more successful if you read the recipe well, and extract from it as much information as you can before you start cooking. This must be done well in advance so that shopping can be organized and any pre-preparation — such as marinating, soaking of pulses and dried fruit, making stock and pastries that need a certain amount of chilling — can be carried out.

Start by reading the list of ingredients. Check that you have all the ingredients to hand before you start cooking and, to save time, weigh out the required quantities. Always use either metric or imperial weights, *never* combine the two. Make sure that you understand all the terminology in the method — now is the time to refer to the listing of cookery terms on p. 216. Allow plenty of time for skills and processes that have to be carried out such as:

♦ trimming and boning of meat
♦ cleaning, filleting and skinning of fish
♦ peeling and chopping of vegetables and fruit
♦ soaking of gelatine

The annotation that accompanies the specimen recipes shown here provides a few examples of the kind of specific detail that should be looked for when reading a recipe. A prerequisite for thoroughness is time — if you always allow yourself that and pay attention to detail, you will almost certainly guarantee a good result.

You must also allow time for basics such as the cooking itself as well as cooling, setting and freezing, whichever is appropriate. Time must also be taken into account for finishing dishes — for example, making sauces, and for garnishing and decorating.

If all these suggestions are followed, cooking should become more pleasurable because the pressure and anxiety that comes with disorganized working methods has been removed. In order to achieve first-class results, great care must be taken in the basic preparations.

FIRST COURSE: CONSOMME JULIENNE This recipe is a good example of one which looks straightforward enough but has hidden pitfalls to catch the unwary. Insufficient care when straining the liquid will result in a cloudy consommé. Note too that the utensils used for this operation should be clean and grease free.

CONSOMME JULIENNE

CLEAR SOUP WITH VEGETABLE GARNISH

Remove the fat and shred the meat finely. Place in a pan with the stock, vegetables, bouquet garni, tomato, salt and black pepper and the egg whites lightly beaten with the water. Bring slowly to simmering point, stirring all the time. When it begins to cloud, stir very gently until it boils.

Reduce the heat and simmer for 20-30 minutes until a crust has formed and the liquid is clear and brilliant. Strain through a clean muslin cloth into a perfectly clean bowl. Add the sherry and the julienne strips and pour into a warmed tureen.

♦ Great care must be taken not to mix the crust with the liquid when straining the consommé or the result will be cloudy. All utensils must be clean and grease free.

INGREDIENTS

To Serve 4-6

350g/12oz shin of beef

1.2lt/2pt brown stock (see page 68)

1 carrot, finely chopped

1 leek, finely chopped

1 stick of celery, finely chopped

bouquet garni

1 tomato, quartered

salt

black pepper

4 egg whites

120ml/4fl oz water

2 tbsp sherry

julienne strips of carrot, turnip and French beans

Bouchees A La Reine

PUFF PASTRY CASES FILLED WITH CHICKEN AND MUSHROOM

The bouchée was created for Marie Leszcinska, gourmet queen of Louis XV.

Roll out the puff pastry on a lightly floured board to a 33cm/13 inch square. Cut out 16 circles 7.5cm/3 inches diameter and brush lightly with the beaten egg. With the back of a small knife, mark the circles with a lattice pattern and cut the centres neatly from 8 of them with a 4.5cm/1¾ inch cutter. Place the whole circles on a dampened baking sheet, put a circle with its centre removed on each one and press down firmly. Place in a refrigerator to chill for 20 minutes.

Bake for 15-20 minutes, then carefully remove the round of pastry that rises through the centre and keep this for a lid. With a teaspoon, scoop out any soft pastry from inside the bouchées. Reduce the temperature to 190°C/375°F/Gas Mark 5 and return the bouchées to the oven for 5-7 minutes to dry out. Reserve the lids until the bouchées are filled.

Melt half the butter in a small pan, add the flour and cook for 3-4 minutes. Remove from the heat and stir in the stock a little at a time. Bring to the boil stirring all the time and cook for a further 4-5 minutes.

Heat the remaining butter in a clean pan, and add the mushrooms, lemon juice, salt and black pepper. Cook until tender and drain well. Add the mushrooms and chicken to the sauce, reheat, taste and adjust the seasoning.

Fill the bouchées with the mushroom and chicken mixture, replace the lids and serve hot.

INGREDIENTS
To Serve 4

Pâte feuilletée made with 225g/8oz strong flour (see page 70)

beaten egg to glaze

50g/2oz butter

25g/1oz flour

300ml/½pt chicken stock

50g/2oz mushrooms, thinly sliced

1 tsp lemon juice

salt

black pepper

225g/8oz shredded cooked chicken

Pre-heat the oven to 230°C/450°F/Gas Mark 8.

Salade Aux Noix

GREEN SALAD WITH NUTS

(Franche-Comté)

Cut the pepper in half, discard the seeds and pith, and cut into fine shreds. Blanch in boiling salted water for 1 minute, drain and refresh in cold water.

Place the lettuce leaves, pepper and nuts in a salad bowl, add the chopped herbs to the vinaigrette and, just before serving, toss the salad in this.

INGREDIENTS
To Serve 4-6

1 green pepper

1 large round lettuce, washed and dried

25g/1oz walnuts, chopped

2 tbsp chopped fresh herbs

Sauce vinaigrette (see page 65)

Bavarois Rubane

A LAYERED DESSERT WITH THREE FLAVOURS

Chill a 13cm/5 inch charlotte tin. Melt the chocolate in a bowl over a pan of hot water. Soak the gelatine in cold water.

Warm the milk in a small pan. Put the egg yolks, sugar and arrowroot in a bowl and mix well. Pour on the milk, return to the pan and stir over a gentle heat until the custard thickens without boiling. Remove from the heat and stir in the gelatine.

Divide the custard into three portions. Add the melted chocolate to one portion, the vanilla sugar to the second and the kirsch to the third. Colour the third pink with the carmine. Leave until on the point of setting. Whisk the cream until it forms soft peaks and fold a third of it into each portion of custard.

Put the pink kirsch-flavoured custard in the mould and place over ice until this has set. Cover with the vanilla-flavoured custard and leave to set as before. Finally, cover with the chocolate custard and chill until required.

Loosen the edge of the bavarois by easing it away from the mould with the fingertips. Dip the mould into hot water for 2-3 seconds and turn out onto a serving dish.

INGREDIENTS
To Serve 4-6

100g/4oz chocolate

5 leaves of gelatine

600ml/1pt milk

6 egg yolks

75g/3oz sugar

a pinch of arrowroot

4 tsp vanilla sugar

4 tbsp kirsch

carmine colouring

300ml/½pt double cream

MAIN COURSE: BOUCHEES A LA REINE *An important skill is needed here — making pâte feuilletée — so ensure that you familiarize yourself with the more intricate steps in this process. Timing is also an important consideration. For example, if the bouchées are to be served hot, make sure that you allow sufficient time for the various stages in their preparation.*

VEGETABLES: SALADE AUX NOIX *A straightforward and quick to prepare salad, but note that the pepper should be cut into fine shreds before being blanched in boiling salted water. Don't forget to check that you have walnuts in stock, for the dish has no point without them.*

DESSERTS: BAVAROIS RUBANE *Kirsch makes a useful contribution to many desserts, and this one is no exception, so ensure that you have some. Make sure too that you have a charlotte tin of the requisite size. There are several vital stages in this recipe which necessitate care and attention. For example, chilling the charlotte tin, soaking the gelatine and placing the custard-filled mould over ice are operations that can slip the mind if careful note is not made of them, and the inexperienced or careless could end up boiling the milk rather than warming it.*

REGIONAL WINES

The wines of France are renowned throughout the world, and often the finest complement for a good French dish is a good French wine. And, as the recipes from the regions differ in ingredients and combinations, so the regional wines proclaim their individual characters and flavours. We have listed below many of the principal wines of the regions, along with a guide to which foods they will usually best accompany.

Although the wine chosen to complement a meal is ultimately a matter of personal taste (as well as of budget), in general there are a few rules. White wines are the best to drink with fish, and they could also accompany lighter meats such as poultry, pork or veal (as could rosé). The stronger red wines will best accompany the more flavourful meats such as beef, lamb or game. The sweet heavy wines, such as Sauternes, should really only be served with desserts.

Always try to serve a local wine when cooking a regional dish, and remember that the best drink with which to accompany a dish which has a wine in its sauce, is the wine used in the cooking.

SERVING WINE

Having chosen the correct wine to accompany your meal, it is most important that you serve it in the right order — white before red, dry before sweet, light before heavy, young before old — and at the appropriate temperature.

Wines should be brought slowly to the correct temperature. Dry white and rosé wines should be served chilled between 46°F/8°C and 54°F/12°C. Sweet white wines, champagne or sparkling wines may be served even cooler, at between 43°F/6°C and 46°F/8°C. Light and fruity wines should be served at cellar temperature — between 50°F/10°C and 54°F/12°C — and other red wines at room temperature, at between 61°F/16°C and 66°F/19°C. Never put wine in the deep freeze to chill it quickly — if left too long the bottle will explode. To chill the wine quickly the bottle should be placed in an ice bucket filled with ice and cold water, but ideally white wine should chill in the refrigerator for about 2 hours. Red wine should not be place in hot water to bring to room temperature nor should it be put on a radiator or in a microwave cooker. The bottle should simply be left at room temperature for about 2 hours. To be enjoyed at their best, wines should be brought slowly to their correct serving temperature. If service is required quickly, red wine may be decanted to a warmed decanter.

BRITTANY

Muscadet. A crisp, dry white wine.
Gros Plant. Similar to Muscadet, slightly less expensive but a good buy.
Served with shellfish, particularly oysters, deep-fried fish, whitebait, sprats, sardines, moules à la marinière.

LYONNAIS

Beaujolais. A light-bodied red wine drunk young and cool.
Served with roasted or grilled beef or pork, kidneys in a cream sauce, blanquettes, fricassées, vegetables and gammon.
Côteaux de Lyonnais. A rich sweet white wine.
Served with desserts.

ILE DE FRANCE

Champagne. Usually white but a pink variety is available — ranging from dry to sweet.
Can be served as an aperitif, all through a meal, on special occasions, with turbot, fish quenelles, oysters. Sweet champagne with Christmas pudding, crêpes suzettes.

PROVENCE

Côte de Provence. A reliable solid dry wine which can be red or white, or sometimes rosé.
Moussaka. Red with blue cheeses.

ANJOU

Vouvray. White — ranging from crisp dry to those with a fuller flavour.
Sweet Vouvray with soufflés, strawberries and cream, cheesecake. Dry Vouvray with poached salmon and plain trout.
Sauvennière. Vigorous full-bodied white.
Served with vegetables 'au gratin'.
Saumur Mousseux. Sparkling white wine made by the champagne method — very good value.
Served with desserts and fruit.

ALSACE

Gewürztraminer. Spicy white wine with a touch of sweetness.
Served with pâtés, scallops, lobster, smoked salmon, stuffed trout or trout with a rich sauce, Munster cheese, sweet tarts, soufflés and crêpes.
Muscat. White wine — ranging from crisp to soft in flavour.
Served as an aperitif with canapés. Stewed fruits, Kugelhopf or cheese.
Riesling. A full-bodied white wine with a touch of sweetness.
Served with cold lobster, scallops and all shellfish. Spring chicken, teal, wild duck, roast rabbit or hare, choucroûte.
Pinot Noir. A light-bodied non-tannic red wine.
To serve with chicken with spicy accompaniments, game casseroles and red meats.

NORMANDY

Not renowned for its wine. The local drink is cider.

BURGUNDY

Sancerre. A crisp white wine.
Goes particularly well with goat's cheese, hot lobster, sole served with a sauce, foie gras, teal and wild duck.
Pouilly Fumé. Full-bodied crisp white wine.
Served as an aperitif or with shellfish, foie gras.
Chablis. A crisp, muscular, full-bodied white wine.
Served with oysters, salmon with a heavy sauce, teal and wild duck.
Meursault. A complex deep white wine.
Served with fish, shellfish, oysters and other sea foods.
Corton Charlemagne. A complex, deep white wine.
Goes particularly well with foie gras.

LANGUEDOC

Minervois. A red wine which is lively and full of flavour.
Served with stews, casseroles and hamburgers.
Corbières. A fruity red wine which is moderately robust.
Served with cassoulet, moussaka, tripe, hamburgers, stews and casseroles.
Roussillon. A dry light-bodied red wine.
Served with desserts and fruit and English cheeses.
Blanquet de Limoux. A sparkling wine made by the champagne method — very good value.
Served with shellfish, oysters, fish and other sea foods.

PAYS BASQUE AND THE SOUTH-WEST

Entre-Deux-Mers. A crisp semi-sweet white wine.
Served with shellfish, oysters, fish and other sea foods.
Sauternes. A light sweet white wine.
Served with fruit flans, strawberries and cream, crème brûlée, summer pudding.
St Emilion. A big complex fine red wine.
Served with light meats roasted and grilled, duck, goose, pheasant, grouse, woodcock and other small game birds and venison.
Bergerac. A soft fruity red wine.
Served at a luncheon with light meats or barbecued food, or with roast beef.

FRANCHE-COMTE

Châteauneuf du Pape. A big, robust, complex red wine.
Served with waterbirds such as teal and wild duck, roast rabbit and hare, venison and English cheeses.
Hermitage. A fine deep red wine, also a vigorous muscular white wine.
Served with shellfish, oysters, fish and other sea foods, boeuf stroganoff, T-bone steak, English cheeses and blue cheeses.

The Côte de Beaune is one of the best known areas in the world for dry white wines. Domaine Leflaive (opposite) is the most famous estate in this area. Here they pick the noble Chardonnay grapes, and with the skill and expertise which has been passed down through the generations of the Leflaive family, produce wines with a flavour and bouquet that makes the tasting an experience that all serious wine drinkers will agree should not be missed.

THE RECIPES

The selection of recipes that follows
to both the regional and classical
The *Basic Preparations*, covering
will provide the essential secrets to
recipes, which can be served as light
the wide range of provincial poultry,
the *Main Course* section. The versatile
included here are ideal as accompani—
manner, as a separate course. The
options, from the simple and light to
there are the *Classics*, dishes which
special occasions.

will serve as the perfect introduction

cookery of France.

sauces, dressings and pastry recipes,

many French dishes. The *First Course*

main courses, are superb appetizers for

meat, fish and egg dishes that form

and imaginative *Vegetable* recipes

ments or, in the traditional French

Desserts, too, offer several delicious

the indulgently rich. And, finally,

are a gourmet's delight for those

BASIC PREPARATIONS

The recipes included in this chapter are those which can be found in every cookery book and form the basis of a wide variety of techniques. The basic recipes that we have included are well tried and tested and can be easily followed. As you become familiar with them they can be adapted to suit any recipe.

BEURRE MANIE

Put the butter and flour on a plate and work them together with a fork until a smooth paste is obtained. This mixture keeps well in the refrigerator until required.

To use, small pieces of the paste are whisked or stirred briskly into boiling liquid until the required thickness is reached. It is important that all the starch in the flour is cooked or the flavour will be spoilt.

INGREDIENTS

50g/2oz butter

50g/2oz flour

SAUCE DEMI-GLACE

Heat the dripping in a heavy pan, and fry the bacon until golden brown. Remove the bacon from the fat and keep on one side. Add the onion and carrot to the fat and cook slowly until they are beginning to turn golden brown — this process cannot be hurried or the vegetables will scorch. Sprinkle in the flour and cook over a low heat, stirring occasionally, for 15 minutes or until it is a rich brown.

Add the stock, bacon, mushrooms, salt and black pepper and bring to the boil, stirring all the time. Simmer uncovered for 30 minutes. Stir in the tomato purée and sherry and cook for 15-20 minutes. Put through a fine conical sieve, taste and adjust the seasoning and reheat before using as required.

INGREDIENTS

50g/2oz dripping or lard

50g/2oz bacon, cut into lardons

1 small onion, finely chopped

1 small carrot, finely chopped

2 tbsp flour

450ml/$\frac{3}{4}$pt brown stock (see page 68)

100g/4oz mushrooms, finely chopped

salt

black pepper

2 tsp tomato purée

2 tbsp sherry

SAUCE VINAIGRETTE

Put the vinegar, salt, black pepper, sugar and the mustard in a small bowl and add the oil slowly, whisking all the time. If preferred, place all the ingredients in a screw-top jar and shake well to mix. Use as required.

INGREDIENTS

2 tbsp wine vinegar

salt

black pepper

a pinch of sugar

$\frac{1}{4}$ tsp Dijon mustard

6 tbsp olive oil

65

Sauce MAYONNAISE

INGREDIENTS

2 egg yolks

½tsp Dijon mustard

a pinch of sugar

white pepper

300ml/½pt olive oil

2-3 tbsp wine vinegar

¼ tsp salt

Put the egg yolks, mustard, sugar and white pepper in a bowl and beat until they thicken slightly. Drip the oil in a little at a time, beating continuously. When the mixture starts to thicken and a good emulsion is formed, the oil may be added a little more quickly — if it becomes very thick and difficult to beat, add some of the vinegar.

Once all the oil has been added, mix in the remaining vinegar and the salt. Taste and adjust the seasoning. Use as required.

♦ The consistency of the mayonnaise may be adjusted by adding a little boiling water.

If the mayonnaise should curdle it can be rectified and should not be thrown away. Put a fresh egg yolk into a clean basin and drip the curdled mayonnaise onto this, beating all the time.

Sauce BECHAMEL

INGREDIENTS

25g/1oz butter

25g/1oz flour

300ml/½pt milk

salt

white pepper

Melt the butter in a small pan, remove from the heat, stir in the flour and cook for 2-3 minutes, stirring all the time. Remove from the heat and add the milk a little at a time. Bring to the boil, stirring continuously, then simmer for 3-4 minutes. Season with salt and white pepper, and use as required.

♦ For a sauce with a thicker consistency, 40g/1½oz butter and flour should be used to 300ml/½pt milk.

Aspic Jelly

Soak the gelatine in cold water.

Place the stock, vegetables, bouquet garni, tomato, gelatine, salt, black pepper and the egg whites lightly beaten with the water in a large saucepan and bring slowly to simmering point, stirring all the time. When it begins to cloud stir very gently until it boils.

Reduce the heat and simmer for 20-30 minutes until a crust has formed and the liquid is clear and brilliant. Strain through a clean muslin cloth into a clean bowl and stir in the sherry. Use as required.

♦ Great care must be taken not to mix the crust with the liquid when straining the aspic or the result will be cloudy. All utensils must be clean and grease free.

INGREDIENTS

10 leaves of gelatine
1.2lt/2pt stock, white or brown (see page 68)
1 leek, finely chopped
1 stick of celery, finely chopped
bouquet garni
1 tomato, quartered
salt
black pepper
4 egg whites
120ml/4fl oz water
2 tbsp sherry

If the aspic is to be used with fish, the method of making it will be exactly the same but the ingredients are as specified in the column below right.

10 leaves of gelatine
1.2lt/2pt fish stock (see page 68)
1 leek, finely chopped
bouquet garni
a sprig of fennel
a sprig of tarragon
salt
black pepper
4 egg whites
150ml/$\frac{1}{4}$pt white wine

Court Bouillon

Simmer all the ingredients together for 45 minutes, strain and cool before using as required.

INGREDIENTS

1lt/1$\frac{3}{4}$pt water
bouquet garni
$\frac{1}{2}$ onion, sliced
$\frac{1}{2}$ carrot, sliced
1 tsp salt
4 peppercorns
300ml/$\frac{1}{2}$pt dry white wine or 25ml/1fl oz wine vinegar

FISH STOCK

bones of 2 or 3 sole

1 onion, sliced

1 carrot, sliced

bouquet garni

1.75lt/3pt water

Wash the bones thoroughly, and place them in a large pan with the vegetables, bouquet garni and the water. Bring slowly to the boil, remove any scum that rises to the surface, reduce the heat, and simmer uncovered for 20 minutes. Strain and use as required.

♦ It is important not to cook the stock for longer than the stated time as it will become bitter.

Other fish bones may be substituted but never use plaice bones, as these will make a bitter stock.

VEGETABLE STOCK

INGREDIENTS

1 carrot, chopped

1 leek, chopped

1 small onion, chopped

1 stick of celery, chopped

bouquet garni

900ml/$1\frac{1}{2}$pt water

$\frac{1}{2}$ level tsp salt

Place all the ingredients in a large pan and bring to the boil. Boil gently for 30 minutes, strain and use as required.

WHITE STOCK

INGREDIENTS

veal or beef bones or chicken carcass

1 carrot

1 onion

1 leek

2 sticks of celery

bouquet garni

Place the bones in a large pan, cover with cold water, bring slowly to the boil and remove any scum that rises to the surface. Reduce the heat, add the vegetables and bouquet garni, cover with a lid and simmer gently for 4-5 hours, skimming the liquid occasionally. Strain and use as required.

♦ For brown stock, place the bones and an extra carrot and onion in a roasting pan in a very hot oven (230°C/450°F/Gas Mark 8), and cook until well browned before boiling as above.

PATE A CHOUX

Sift the flour onto a piece of greaseproof paper. Put the butter and water in a medium sized pan and warm until the butter has melted. Bring to the boil, shoot all the flour in at once and beat quickly — keep the pan over the heat for 1 minute if necessary — until the mixture thickens to a smooth glossy paste which leaves the sides of the pan.

Add the egg yolk, mix well and gradually add the egg, beating continuously. The mixture should be thick and shiny. Use as required.

INGREDIENTS
50g/2oz strong flour
25g/1oz butter
150ml/¼pt water
1 egg yolk
1 egg, beaten

PATE SUCREE

Sift the flour onto a board, make a well in the centre and add the butter, sugar and egg yolks. Work with the fingertips so that the butter and egg yolks are first rubbed into the flour and sugar and then worked together to form a ball of dough — the dough must be smooth and pliable, not at all crumbly.

Wrap in greaseproof paper or cling film and put aside to chill for 20-30 minutes in the refrigerator. Use as required.

INGREDIENTS
150g/5oz plain flour
75g/3oz butter
50g/2oz caster sugar
2 egg yolks

PATE DEMI-FEUILLETEE

FLAKY PASTRY

Sift the flour and salt into a bowl, add half the butter and rub it in with the fingertips until the mixture resembles fine breadcrumbs. Add 6 tablespoons of the water to the flour and blend lightly together with a round bladed knife. Complete mixing with the hand, adding the remaining water as necessary to make a soft but not sticky dough.

Roll out the dough on a lightly floured board to make an oblong — it is important that the ends are kept square and the sides straight. Mark the oblong of dough lightly into thirds and dot the top two-thirds with half of the lard. Fold the bottom third — with no fat on — up to cover the middle third and the top third down to enclose all the fat. Seal the edges lightly with the rolling pin. Give the pastry a quarter turn so the join is now to the right hand side. Roll again to an oblong and repeat as before, but using the remaining butter. Fold and roll again, this time using the remaining lard. Fold and roll once more then fold without any fat being added.

Wrap in cling film or greaseproof paper and chill for 20-30 minutes before use.

INGREDIENTS
225g/8oz plain flour
a pinch of salt
75g/3oz butter, chilled
75g/3oz lard, chilled
cold water to mix, approx. 1 tbsp per 25g/1oz flour

PATE FEUILLETEE

250g/9oz strong flour

a pinch of salt

150ml/¼pt water

225g/8oz butter

• *See pages 30~31 for step-by-step illustrations*

PUFF PASTRY

Sift the flour and salt onto a pastry board and make a large well in the centre about 15cm/6 inches in diameter. Pour half the water into the well and using the fingertips work in a third of the flour from the sides very gradually — the mixture should not flow together when a finger is drawn through it. Use the fingertips of both hands, palms upwards, and flake the dry flour through the mixture in the centre. Repeat this from all sides of the well — the pastry will look dry and flaky.

Sprinkle half the remaining water over the pastry and flake again, repeat with the rest of the water and form the mixture into a ball and knead lightly — this process is known as making a 'détrempe'. Wrap the dough in cling film and allow to chill for 20 minutes.

Place the détrempe on a lightly floured board and roll to a circle 25cm/10 inches in diameter.

Soften the butter by tapping it with a rolling pin on a piece of greaseproof paper to elongate it, cut in half, put the two pieces of butter together and repeat until the butter is pliable but still cold. Reform to a rectangle approximately 10 x 15cm/4 x 6 inches. Place the butter in the middle of the dough and fold over the dough from the right and left to cover the dough — it should overlap by about 2.5cm/1 inch. Press the dough with a rolling pin to elongate it and mark lightly into three. Fold the bottom third up to cover the middle third and the top third down — the dough is now known as a 'pâton'. Seal the edges gently with the rolling pin and give the dough a quarter turn.

Roll the pastry to a rectangle approximately 18 x 38cm/7 x 15inches — it is important that the ends are kept square and the sides straight. Mark the rectangle of dough lightly into thirds, fold the bottom third up to cover the middle third and the top third down. Seal the edges gently and give the pastry a quarter turn. Repeat the rolling and folding once more then chill the pastry for 20 minutes or until it is firm and cold — the pastry has now had two rollings and foldings. Repeat this process until it has had six rollings and foldings in all.

Chill for 1 hour before use.

♦ Before chilling the pastry, it can be marked with the fingertips to indicate the number of rollings and foldings it has had.

PATE BRISEE

Sift the flour, sugar and salt onto a board, make a well in the centre and add the butter and egg. Work with the fingertips so that the butter and egg are first rubbed into the flour and then worked together to form a ball of dough.

Wrap in greaseproof paper or cling film and put aside to chill for 20-30 minutes in the refrigerator. Use as required.

INGREDIENTS

225g/8oz plain flour

15g/½oz caster sugar (for sweet dishes only)

a pinch of salt

100g/4oz butter

1 egg

• *See page 33 for step-by-step illustration*

CREME CHANTILLY

Place all the ingredients in a bowl which should be standing in a larger bowl containing ice and cold water. Whisk until the cream thickens — it should form soft peaks. Use as required.

Pommes De Terre

INGREDIENTS *Duchesse*

750g/1½lb old potatoes, peeled

25g/1oz butter

2 egg yolks

a pinch of nutmeg

salt

black pepper

PRALINE

Rinse the almonds to remove the powdery substance clinging to the skins. Put the sugar and water into a small pan and stir over a gentle heat until the sugar has dissolved. Raise the heat, add the almonds and boil until the syrup turns a rich brown colour — do not stir while it is boiling or the syrup may crystallize.

To test if the syrup is ready, drop a little into cold water — it should set quickly and be crisp to bite. If using a sugar thermometer, it should be 200°C/400°F. Pour onto an oiled baking sheet and allow to cool completely. Crush and store in an airtight container.

Creme Chantilly

INGREDIENTS

150ml/¼pt double cream

2 tbsp milk

1 level tsp vanilla sugar

POMMES DE TERRE DUCHESSE

Cut the potatoes into even sized pieces, place in a pan of cold salted water, bring to the boil and cook until tender.

Drain well and put them through a metal sieve or vegetable mill into a hot basin. Beat in the butter, egg yolks, nutmeg, salt and black pepper and continue beating until the mixture is very creamy.

Put the mixture into a piping bag with a large rosette nozzle and pipe.

Praline

INGREDIENTS

100g/4oz unblanched almonds

100g/4oz sugar

4 tbsp water

71

FIRST COURSE

When choosing a first course remember that it will be an introduction to the meal and should, therefore, set the standard of the food to follow.

A light consommé or soup will stimulate the appetite and start the flow of digestive juices. Hors d'oeuvres are small portions of food which should be dainty, colourful and effectively garnished. If a cold main course is to be served, precede it with a warming first course. If fruit is to be served in further courses, it must be excluded in this course. In the words of the great French chef, Auguste Escoffier, hors d'oeuvres should 'beguile the consumer's attention and fancy from the very moment of his entering the dining room'.

◆

Mousse au Jambon, a creamy ham mousse; recipe page 74.

Piperade Basquaise

SCRAMBLED EGGS WITH PEPPERS AND TOMATOES
(Pays Basque and the South-West)

The name Pipérade comes from 'piper' (hot red pepper).

INGREDIENTS

To Serve 4

1 large red pepper

1 large green pepper

750g/1½lb small tomatoes

oil for frying

1 clove of garlic, crushed

salt

black pepper

a pinch of sugar

6 eggs, beaten

heart shaped croûtons (see page 52)

• *Illustration, page 76*

Cut the peppers in half, discard the seeds and pith, and chop flesh finely. Cook in boiling salted water for 5-7 minutes, then drain on kitchen paper. Reserve 3 tomatoes and skin, pip and quarter the remainder.

Heat 4-6 tablespoons of oil in a pan, put in the peppers and cook them slowly for 3-4 minutes. Add the quartered tomatoes, garlic, salt, black pepper and sugar, cover the pan and cook for a further 10-15 minutes. Slice the remaining tomatoes and cook them separately and gently in 4-6 tablespoons of oil for a few minutes.

When the pepper and tomato mixture is cooked, pour off any excess liquid, add the eggs and return the pan to a low heat. Stir with a wooden spoon until the eggs are just beginning to set.

Serve in a hot dish garnished with the slices of tomato and the croûtons.

Mousse au Jambon

A CREAMY HAM MOUSSE
(Pays Basque and the South-West)

INGREDIENTS

To Serve 4-6

225g/8oz lean ham

25g/1oz butter

300ml/½pt Aspic jelly, cold but liquid (see page 67)

150ml/¼pt Sauce béchamel (see page 66)

salt

white pepper

a pinch of paprika

150ml/¼pt double cream

1 hardboiled egg

a few blanched tarragon leaves or the green part of a leek

• *Illustration, page 72*

Chill a 13cm/5 inch soufflé dish.

Mince or chop the ham very finely and then pound it, using a pestle and mortar — or put it in a food processor. Cream the butter and mix with the ham. Add about 3 tablespoons of liquid aspic extremely slowly, mixing in only about 1 teaspoon at a time or it will curdle. Add the Sauce béchamel, salt, white pepper and paprika. Whip the cream fairly stiffly and fold in lightly. Taste and adjust the seasoning. Pour the mixture into the mould and smooth over the top. Cover with a thin layer of aspic and leave to set.

Cut the egg white into a lily design and use blanched tarragon or the green part of a leek for the leaves. Arrange the decoration on top of the mousse. Coat with a second layer of aspic and chill for a further half an hour. Serve very cold.

♦ If a very smooth mousse is required, the ham and butter mixture may be sieved. Depending on the type of ham, it may not be necessary to use much salt.

PATE LORRAINE EN CROUTE

RAISED GAME PIE

(Alsace and Lorraine)

Make the pastry first. Sift the flour and salt onto a board. Make a well in the centre and put in all the other ingredients. Mix together and gradually work in the flour, then knead well. Continue kneading until the pastry feels rubbery and elastic. This develops the gluten in the flour and makes it strong enough to hold the filling later.

Relax the pastry for 2 hours or overnight in a cold place. This pastry should not be made in a food processor.

Cut the flesh of the hare or other game into thin strips.

To make the farce, chop any trimmings and mix these with the pork, veal, salt, black pepper, cinnamon and cayenne pepper. Cut the bacon into strips and mix with the onion, parsley and wine. Season with black pepper.

Grease and flour a raised pie mould. Cut off a quarter of the pastry for the lid, roll out the remaining pastry on a lightly floured board and line into the mould. Fill with half of the farce, then place the fillets of hare on top of this, then the bacon and onion mixture. Cover with the rest of the farce and press down well. Fold the edges of the pastry inwards and moisten with beaten egg. Roll out the pastry for the lid, place on the pie and seal the edges well.

Make a hole in the centre to allow the steam to escape and decorate with pastry leaves. Brush with beaten egg and bake for approximately $1\frac{1}{2}$ hours or until the liquid appearing in the opening is clear, with no drops of blood.

When the pie is completely cold, remove from the mould and fill, through the hole in the top, with cool Aspic jelly.

INGREDIENTS

To Serve 6-8

2 joints of hare or other game

350g/12oz pork, minced

350g/12oz veal, minced

1½ level tsp salt

black pepper

a small pinch of cinnamon

a pinch of cayenne pepper

75g/3oz lean bacon

1 onion, finely chopped

1 tsp finely chopped parsley

3 tsp white wine

beaten egg to glaze

300ml/½pt Aspic jelly (see page 67)

Pâte à pâtes

250g/9oz plain flour

1 tsp salt

40g/1½oz lard

75g/3oz butter

4-5 tbsp water

3 tbsp oil

1 egg yolk

Pre-heat the oven to 200°C/ 400°F/Gas Mark 6.

• Illustration, page 92

Pipérade Basquaise, hot scrambled eggs, garnished with sliced tomato and heart-shaped croûtons; recipe page 74.

GALETTES DE SARRASIN

To Serve 6-8

450g/1lb buckwheat flour

2 eggs, lightly beaten

300ml/½pt dry cider

450-600ml/¾-1pt water

225g/8oz butter, melted

½ tsp salt

oil

BUCKWHEAT PANCAKES WITH EGG, HAM, CHEESE AND ONIONS

(Brittany)

Put the flour in a large bowl, make a well in the centre, and add the eggs and half the cider. Mix together, drawing the flour in gradually from the sides of the bowl, adding the rest of the cider and the water until you obtain a smooth fluid batter. Add half of the butter and the salt, mix well and leave to rest at room temperature for 2-3 hours or until required.

Lightly oil a heavy galetoire or frying pan and heat until very hot. Cover the base of the pan with a thin layer of the batter. Cook for 2 minutes, turn the galette over and brush the cooked side with some of the remaining melted butter. Cook the second side for a moment or so, then add the filling as required. Fold the galette in half, brush again with butter and fold in half again to serve.

Re-oil the pan after cooking each galette.

FILLINGS

Egg and ham Break an egg onto the galette and spread over the surface, breaking the yolk. Place a small slice of cooked ham on this and sprinkle with grated cheese, if liked.

Onions and tomatoes Spread a thin layer of cooked onions and tomatoes on the galette.

Onions and cheese Spread a thin layer of cooked onions on the galette and sprinkle with cheese.

Mushrooms and bacon Spread a thin layer of cooked mushrooms on the galette and cover with 1 or 2 cooked rashers of bacon.

A combination of any of the above may be used.

QUICHE ALSACIENNE

A LEEK AND HAM FLAN

(Alsace and Lorraine)

Clean the leeks and slice thinly into rings. Melt the butter in a pan and sweat the leeks until tender. Add the ham.

Roll out the Pâte brisée on a lightly floured board and line into an 18cm/7 inch flan ring. Put the leek and ham mixture in the pastry case and cover with the cheese. Whisk the eggs lightly and beat in the milk or cream. Season with the cayenne pepper, salt and black pepper and strain the mixture into the flan.

Cook for 10 minutes, then reduce the temperature to 180°C/350°F/ Gas Mark 4 for a further 25-30 minutes or until set and golden brown.

INGREDIENTS

To Serve 4

2 medium leeks

50g/2oz butter

75g/3oz ham, coarsely chopped

Pâte brisée made with 100g/ 4oz plain flour (see page 71)

75g/3oz cheese, thinly sliced

2 eggs

150ml/¼pt milk or single cream

a pinch of cayenne pepper

salt

black pepper

Pre-heat the oven to 220°C/ 425°F/Gas Mark 7.

● *See page 33 for step-by-step illustrations of how to make Pâte brisée*

FONDUE SAVOYARD

HOT CHEESE AND WINE DIP

(Franche-Comté)

Rub an earthenware pot with the cut clove of garlic and heat the wine and lemon juice in this. Add the cheese gradually, stirring all the time. Blend the kirsch and cornflour together and add to the melted cheese. Stir on a low heat until smooth, add salt and white pepper to taste, and simmer for 1-2 minutes.

Adjust the consistency if necessary: if it is too thick, add a little more wine; if it is too thin, thicken with extra cornflour.

Serve with cubes of French bread which should be dipped in the fondue with long forks. Keep the fondue hot over a gentle heat — a special pan and burner can be used.

INGREDIENTS

To Serve 4-6

1 clove of garlic

350ml/12fl oz white wine

1 tsp lemon juice

275g/10oz Gruyère cheese, grated

275g/10oz Emmental cheese, grated

2-3 tbsp kirsch

1 tbsp cornflour

salt

white pepper

cubes of French bread

Moules à la Marinière, mussels poached in wine and garnished with parsley; recipe page 94.

ESCARGOTS A LA BOURGUIGNONNE

SNAILS WITH GARLIC BUTTER

(Burgundy)

INGREDIENTS

To Serve 2

12 snails

a pinch of salt

1 dsp vinegar

½ tsp flour

225ml/7½fl oz white wine

225ml/7½fl oz white stock (see page 68)

1 carrot, sliced

1 onion, sliced

1 shallot, sliced

½ tsp salt

bouquet garni

Beurre à la bourguignonne

1 clove of garlic, crushed

2 shallots, chopped

65g/2½oz unsalted butter

1 dsp finely chopped parsley

salt

black pepper

Pre-heat the oven to 200°C/ 400°F/Gas Mark 6

• *Illustration, page 93*

To prepare fresh snails, take off the chalky seal on the shells and wash the snails several times in cold water. Place the snails in a bowl, cover with cold water, add the salt, vinegar and flour, and allow to soak for 2 hours. Wash thoroughly again. Put them in a pan of boiling water and cook for 5 minutes, then drain and take the snails out of their shells. Remove the black part at the end of the tail.

Place the wine, stock, carrot, onion, shallot, salt and bouquet garni in a pan, add the snails, bring to the boil and simmer for 3-4 hours. Leave snails to cool in the stock.

Clean the shells by boiling them in water containing soda crystals for half an hour, then rinse in clean water and drain.

If using a can of snails, ignore the instructions given above. Remove from the brine and drain them well

To make the Beurre à la bourguignonne, place all the ingredients in a mortar and pound to a paste. Put a little butter and a snail in each shell and fill the shell with more butter. Heat through for 10 minutes. Serve at once.

♦ The Beurre à la bourguignonne can be made in a liquidizer or food processor.

GNOCCHI A LA PARISIENNE

A PASTRY CASE FILLED WITH SMALL DUMPLINGS OF CHOUX PASTRY IN A CHEESE SAUCE

(Ile de France and the North)

Roll out the Pâte brisée on a lightly floured board, line into an 18cm/7 inch flan ring, and prick the base well. Bake blind for approximately 20 minutes. When it is cooked, reduce the temperature to 180°C/350°F/Gas Mark 4, remove the paper and beans from the flan case and cook for a further 10 minutes to dry the base.

Place the Pâte à choux in a piping bag with a 1cm/½ inch plain nozzle. Pipe 1cm/½ inch lengths into a pan of boiling salted water, cutting to size with a wet knife. Poach the gnocchi gently for 10 minutes, then lift out carefully with a draining spoon, refresh under the cold tap and drain them.

Melt the butter for the sauce in a small pan. Remove from the heat, stir in the flour and cook for 2-3 minutes. Remove from the heat, and add the milk a little at a time. Bring to the boil, stirring continuously, and simmer for 2-3 minutes. Remove from the heat and whisk in the cheese, salt and white pepper.

Carefully stir the gnocchi into the sauce, and pour into the flan case. Sprinkle with the cheese and dot with butter. Brown under a hot grill or in the top of a hot oven. Serve at once.

INGREDIENTS

To Serve 6

Pâte brisée made with 100g/4oz plain flour (see page 71)

Pâte à choux made with 100g/4oz strong flour (see page 69)

Sauce Mornay

25g/1oz butter

25g/1oz flour

300ml/½pt milk

50g/2oz Cheddar cheese, grated

salt

white pepper

To finish

25g/1oz Cheddar cheese, grated

15g/½oz butter

Pre-heat the oven to 200°C/400°F/Gas Mark 6.

● *See page 33 for step-by-step illustrations of how to make Pâte brisée.*

GOUGERE AU FROMAGE

A LIGHT CHOUX PASTRY RING FLAVOURED WITH CHEESE

(Burgundy)

Wherever 'la gougère' originated, this light cheese pastry as an accompaniment to a glass of Beaujolais makes a delicious aperitif.

Lightly grease a baking sheet and, using a saucepan lid as a guide, trace out a 15cm/6 inch circle.

Make the choux pastry, and add the diced Gruyère cheese to it. Season well with salt and black pepper. Put the mixture into a piping bag with a 2cm/¾ inch plain nozzle, and pipe round the traced ring on the baking sheet. Brush with beaten egg and sprinkle with the finely chopped nuts and slices of Gruyère cheese.

Bake for 10 minutes, then reduce the temperature to 190-200°C/375-400°F/Gas Mark 5-6 for a further 20-25 minutes. Serve at once.

INGREDIENTS

To Serve 4

Pâte à choux made with 50g/2oz strong flour (see page 69)

50g/2oz Gruyère cheese, finely diced

salt

black pepper

beaten egg to glaze

1 tbsp finely chopped almonds

a few wafer-thin slices of Gruyère cheese

Pre-heat the oven to 220-230°C/425-450°F/Gas Mark 7-8

Pissaladière, a bread base
topped with onion and
tomato and decorated with
anchovies and olives;
recipe page 87.

BOUILLABAISSE

INGREDIENTS

To Serve 4-6

2 red mullet

1 sole

450g/1lb turbot

2 mackerel

2 whiting

1 crayfish

3 tbsp olive oil

3 onions, finely chopped

4 leeks, white part only, chopped

4 large tomatoes, skinned, pipped and chopped

4 cloves of garlic, crushed

salt

black pepper

450ml/³/4pt vegetable, white or chicken stock (see page 68)

a pinch of powdered saffron

1 tsp tomato purée

bouquet garni

parsley, chopped

● *See pages 38-39 for step-by-step illustrations of cleaning round and flat fish*

FISH STEW

(Provence)

Gut and scale the fish and cut into 5cm/2 inch lengths.

Heat the oil in a deep pan and cook the onions and leeks for 2-3 minutes. Add the tomatoes, garlic, salt and black pepper and cook for a further 5 minutes. Add the stock, saffron, tomato purée and bouquet garni and bring to the boil.

Stir in the mullet, sole and turbot and cook rapidly for 5 minutes, then add the mackerel, whiting and crayfish and continue to cook for 15 minutes.

Remove the fish and place in a warm dish. Reduce the liquor by half by boiling, pour over the fish and sprinkle with the parsley. Serve with French bread.

♦ Generally the heads are left on the fish in this recipe, but if preferred they may be removed.

PISSALADIERE

A BREAD BASE WITH AN ONION AND TOMATO TOPPING
(Provence)

Sift the flour and salt into a bowl and rub in the butter. Dissolve the yeast in 2 tablespoons of the tepid water, make a well in the centre of the flour and add the egg and yeast. Mix to form a dough, adding more water if required. Cover and leave to rise for 1 hour.

Heat the oil in a frying pan and cook the onions gently until soft but not coloured. Add the tomatoes, salt, black pepper and the garlic. Cook until all the liquid has evaporated and allow to cool.

When the dough has risen, turn out onto a lightly floured board and knead well. Roll into a thin circle, place on a greased baking sheet and cover with the filling. Decorate with a lattice of anchovies and olives and leave to rise in a warm place for 15 minutes. Bake for 15 minutes then reduce the temperature to 180°C/350°F/Gas Mark 4 and cook for a further 15-20 minutes.

INGREDIENTS
To Serve 4

100g/4oz strong flour
¼ tsp salt
25g/1oz butter
15g/½oz yeast
a little tepid water
1 egg, lightly beaten
2-3 tbsp oil
350g/12oz onions, finely sliced
2 tomatoes, skinned and sliced
salt
black pepper
1 clove of garlic, crushed
a few anchovy fillets
black olives

Pre-heat the oven to 200°C/400°F/Gas Mark 6

• *Illustration, page 84*

VELOUTE DE ROQUEFORT

A BLUE CHEESE SOUP
(Languedoc and the Centre)

In 1411 the French king signed a charter granting the inhabitants of Roquefort-sur-Soulzon 'the monopoly of curing cheese as has been done in the caves of the aforesaid village since time immemorial'.

Melt three-quarters of the butter in a large pan and sweat the vegetables over a gentle heat for 7-10 minutes, shaking the pan from time to time. When all the vegetables are soft, remove from the heat and mix in the flour. Return the pan to the heat and cook for 2-3 minutes, stirring all the time. Add the milk, stock, salt and black pepper and simmer for 10 minutes.

Crush the cheese with a fork and mix with the rest of the butter. Remove the soup from the heat, and whisk in the cheese and butter mixture together with the cream. Taste and adjust the seasoning.

Place the bread in a warmed tureen or in individual soup bowls and pour the soup over. Serve at once.

INGREDIENTS
To Serve 6-8

50g/2oz butter
1 medium onion, chopped
1 small head of celery, chopped
1 carrot, chopped
1 clove of garlic, crushed
25g/1oz flour
150ml/¼pt milk
1lt/1¾pt white stock (see page 68)
salt
black pepper
25g/1oz Roquefort cheese
4 tbsp double cream
6-8 small slices of French bread, lightly toasted

Quenelles Nantua, a light
fish mixture with a
shellfish sauce;
recipe page 90.

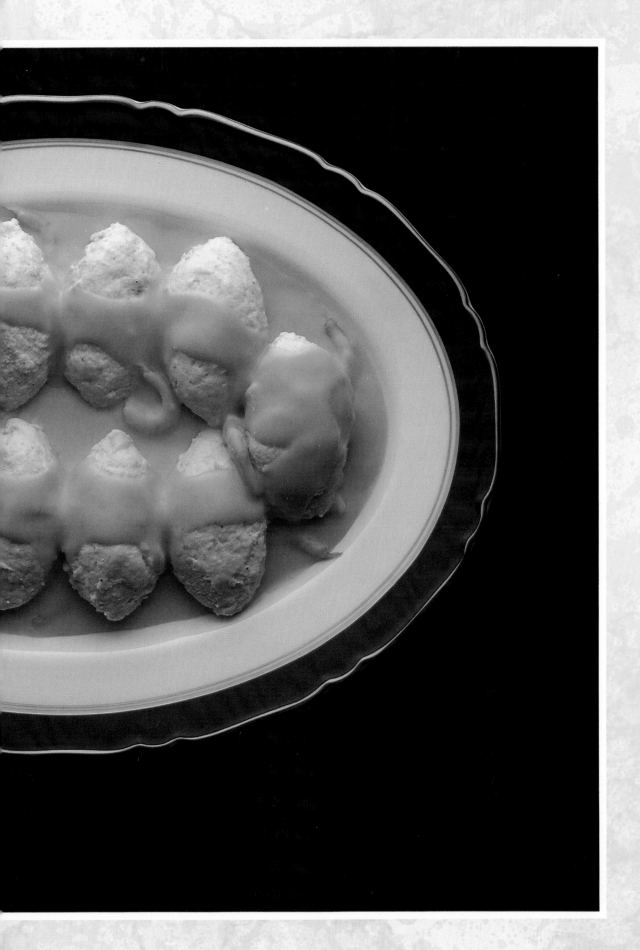

QUENELLES NANTUA

INGREDIENTS

To Serve 4

450g/1lb whiting fillets, skinned

2 egg whites

4 tbsp double cream

salt

white pepper

75g/3oz crayfish or prawns, unshelled

40g/1½oz butter

300ml/½pt thick Sauce béchamel (see page 66)

a pinch of cayenne pepper

carmine colouring

● *Illustration, page 88*

A LIGHT FISH MIXTURE WITH A SHELLFISH SAUCE

(Franche-Comté)

The word 'quenelle' is a derivation of the German 'knödel' meaning dumpling.

To prepare by hand, mince the fish, pound well, adding the egg whites and cream. Season with salt and white pepper.

If using a liquidizer, put the egg whites in first, then add the fish and cream. It is a fairly heavy mixture, so it may have to be made in several batches. Season with salt and white pepper.

If using a food processor, process the fish, and add the egg white and cream slowly while mixing, until all is incorporated. Season with salt and white pepper.

Chill the mixture.

Remove the shells and heads from the crayfish or prawns and reserve the tail flesh. Pound the shells and heads in a pestle and mortar or in a food processor, then add the butter and pound again. Sieve the butter and whisk into the hot Sauce béchamel a little at a time. Taste and adjust the seasoning, adding the cayenne pepper. If necessary, add a few drops of carmine colouring. Finally, add the tail flesh and keep hot.

Form the fish mixture into egg shapes, using 2 tablespoons dipped in hot water. Poach in salted water — it should be simmering, *not boiling* — for 10-15 minutes. Remove carefully and keep warm in a bowl of hot water. When all the quenelles are cooked, drain well and place them in a serving dish and spoon over the sauce. Serve hot.

*Shaping the Quenelles.
Dip two tablespoons in hot water and take a spoonful of the mixture. Form it into an egg shape by scooping the mixture from one spoon to the other.*

SAUCISSON EN BRIOCHE

GARLIC SAUSAGE IN A LIGHT BREAD

(Lyonnais)

Sift the flour onto a pastry board and make a well in the centre. Place the yeast in the well, add 2 tablespoons of warm water and mix the yeast with this using the fingertips. Add the sugar, salt and eggs and mix well working the flour in by degrees from the sides. Continue working for 5 minutes or until the paste becomes elastic, smooth, shiny and lump free. Work in the butter a piece at a time, beating well between each addition.

Put the dough to rise in a warm place in a covered bowl until it has doubled in size. If allowed to get *too* hot whilst rising the butter will melt and run out of the dough. Place in the refrigerator for 2-3 hours or overnight.

Grease a 1kg/2lb loaf tin with melted lard.

Put the dough onto a lightly floured board and knead until it is smooth. Roll the dough to a 23cm/9 inch square and brush with the egg. Place the sausage on the dough, fold over the sides allowing them to overlap in the centre, and seal well. Pinch each end together and place the prepared dough in the tin with the seam underneath. Cover with cling film and allow to rise for 1-2 hours or until the dough has risen to the top of the tin.

Brush with egg and bake for 40-45 minutes or until well brown and shrinking slightly in the tin. Cut into thick slices and serve warm.

INGREDIENTS

To Serve 4-6

225g/8oz strong flour

15g/½oz yeast

15g/½oz caster sugar

1 tsp salt

3 eggs

100g/4oz butter, softened and cut into 2.5cm/1 inch pieces

beaten egg to glaze

450g/1lb French garlic sausage, cooked and skinned

Pre-heat the oven to 200°C/ 400°F/Gas Mark 6

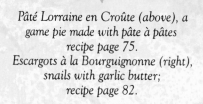

Pâté Lorraine en Croûte (above), a game pie made with pâte à pâtes recipe page 75. Escargots à la Bourguignonne (right), snails with garlic butter; recipe page 82.

Moules a la Mariniere

MUSSELS POACHED IN WINE

(Normandy)

INGREDIENTS

To Serve 4

1.75kg/4lb mussels

2 shallots, finely chopped

1 onion, finely chopped

50g/2oz butter

6 parsley stalks

6 small sprigs of thyme

1 bayleaf

150ml/¼pt dry white wine

black pepper

parsley, finely chopped

Beurre manié, optional (see page 65)

• *Illustration, page 80*

Mussels are cultivated in most coastal regions, usually on wooden posts or bouchots. The word 'marinière' means 'in the boatman's style'.

Prepare the mussels. Any broken mussels must be discarded. If you have one which is open, give it a sharp tap and if it does not close, then the mussel is dead and must not be used as it could cause food poisoning.

When ready to cook the mussels, scrub them very well in several changes of cold water. Scrape off the barnacles with an old knife and also scrape off the beard of the mussel—the black threads on the flat hinge side of the shell. When you have finished cook them immediately.

Place the shallots, onion, butter, herbs, white wine, black pepper and the mussels in a large heavy pan, cover with a lid and shake over a high heat for 5 minutes, or until all the mussels are fully opened. Drain them, reserving the liquor, and remove one shell from each mussel.

Put the mussels in individual serving bowls and pour over the liquor they were cooked in, which can be thickened with Beurre manié if you prefer, and sprinkle generously with the parsley. Serve at once.

♦ If you buy mussels the day before they are needed, put them in a bowl of cold water and sprinkle 2 tablespoons of flour or oats on top. The mussels will feed on this and become plump and tender. In the process, they also clean themselves of sand.

Tarte aux oignons

ONION TART

(Lyonnais)

INGREDIENTS

To Serve 4-6

Pâte demi-feuilletée made with 100g/4oz plain flour (see page 69)

65g/2½oz butter

450g/1lb onions, finely sliced

3 rashers of bacon, diced

40g/1½oz flour

2 eggs

225ml/7½fl oz milk

salt

black pepper

Pre-heat the oven to 200°C/400°F/Gas Mark 6

Roll out the flaky pastry on a lightly floured board, line into an 18cm/7 inch flan ring, and prick the base well.

Melt the butter in a heavy pan, add the onions and the bacon, and cook gently for 15-20 minutes, stirring frequently. Do not allow the onions to colour. Remove from the heat, add the flour and mix well.

Whisk the eggs lightly, add the milk, salt and black pepper and stir into the onion mixture. Pour into the pastry case. Bake for 20-25 minutes and serve hot.

OEUFS A LA TRIPE

HARDBOILED EGGS WITH ONION AND CHEESE SAUCE

(Anjou and the Loire)

This dish — originally from Lavel in Mayenne — earns its name from the strips of hardboiled egg white which could be thought to resemble real tripe.

Cut the egg whites into slices and place in a buttered fireproof dish. Reserve the egg yolks.

Melt the butter in a pan and sweat the onions for 10 minutes. Remove the pan from the heat, stir in the flour, return to the heat and cook for 2-3 minutes, stirring all the time. Pour on the milk, add salt and white pepper, and bring to the boil stirring continuously. Simmer until very thick and creamy, adding more milk if needed.

Remove the sauce from the heat and whisk in the cheese. Taste and adjust the seasoning. Coat the egg whites with the sauce and sieve the egg yolks over the top. Sprinkle with the parsley and serve immediately.

INGREDIENTS

To Serve 4

4 hardboiled eggs

50g/2oz butter

225g/8oz onions, sliced

40g/1½oz flour

300ml/½pt milk

salt

white pepper

50g/2oz Cheddar cheese, grated

2 tbsp finely chopped parsley

SAUMON POCHE AU BEURRE BLANC

POACHED SALMON WITH A SHALLOT AND WINE SAUCE

(Anjou and the Loire)

Poach the salmon cutlets in the Court bouillon for 10 minutes or until the flesh becomes opaque.

For the sauce, place the shallots in a pan with the white wine and 3 tablespoons of the liquid in which the fish was poached. Reduce this by boiling until the shallots are tender and about 2 tablespoons of the liquid remains. Over a very low heat add the softened butter a little at a time, and finally add the cream. Taste and season with salt and white pepper.

Drain the salmon and carefully remove the skin and bone. Place on a warm serving dish and coat with the sauce, which may be sieved if preferred.

♦ If the sauce is overheated, it will separate.

INGREDIENTS

To Serve 4

4 salmon cutlets

600ml/1pt Court bouillon (see page 67)

Sauce beurre blanc
6 shallots, very finely chopped

150ml/¼pt dry white wine

175g/6oz unsalted butter

1 tbsp double cream

salt

white pepper

● Illustration, page 96

95

Saumon Poché au Beurre Blanc, poached salmon with a shallot and wine sauce; recipe page 95.

96

Mousse au Camembert

A LIGHT SAVOURY CAMEMBERT CHEESE MOUSSE

(Normandy)

Camembert cheese is said to have been perfected around 1790 by a farmer's wife, and it is named after a village in the Auge.

INGREDIENTS

To Serve 4-6

3 leaves of gelatine

1 ripe Camembert cheese, 225-250g/8-9oz

50g/2oz butter

25g/1oz flour

300ml/½pt milk

25g/1oz Parmesan cheese, grated

1 tsp tomato purée

1 tsp French mustard

a pinch of cayenne pepper

salt

white pepper

2 eggs, separated

50g/2oz almonds, blanched

Soak the gelatine in cold water. Remove and discard the rind of the Camembert and cream the cheese. Melt half the butter in a small pan and stir in the flour. Cook over a low heat for 1 minute. Remove from the heat, add the milk gradually, bring to the boil and simmer for 5 minutes. Remove from the heat, add the Camembert and Parmesan cheeses, together with the tomato purée, mustard, cayenne pepper, salt, white pepper, gelatine and egg yolks. Return to a low heat and cook, stirring all the time, until it thickens without boiling. Overheating at this stage could cause the mixture to curdle. Pour into a basin and allow to cool.

Put a band of greaseproof paper around a small soufflé dish of about 13cm/5 inches in diameter, and secure with string.

Split the almonds and fry them in the remaining butter. Drain and sprinkle them with salt. Reserve 8-10 for decoration and chop the rest.

When the mixture is on the point of setting, whisk the egg whites until stiff and fold into the mixture. Pour into the prepared soufflé dish and leave in a cool place to set. When firm, remove the greaseproof paper and decorate the edge with the chopped salted almonds. Arrange the split almonds in a pattern in the centre. Serve with toast.

♦ The size of the soufflé dish is important. If it is too large there will be no need for the paper collar as there will not be enough mixture to come above the dish.

Soupe a l'oignon

BROWN ONION SOUP

(Ile de France and the North)

INGREDIENTS

To Serve 4

50g/2oz butter

450g/1lb onions, finely sliced

1 tsp sugar

2 tsp flour

1 lt/1¾pt brown beef stock (see page 68)

salt

black pepper

4 slices of French bread

50g/2oz cheese, grated

Melt the butter in a heavy pan, add the onions and sugar and stir frequently over a moderate heat until the onions are golden brown. This process cannot be hurried and will take about 20 minutes. Stir in the flour and add the stock gradually. Season well with salt and black pepper and simmer gently for 15 minutes.

Cover the bread with the cheese and brown under a hot grill or in the top of a hot oven. Place the bread in a warmed tureen or individual soup bowls and pour the soup over. Serve at once.

Maquereaux Quimper

COLD POACHED MACKEREL WITH A SAVOURY BUTTER

(Brittany)

Place the fish in a shallow pan, cover with the Court bouillon and poach over a very low heat for 15-20 minutes or until they are cooked. Remove from the heat and allow the fish to cool in the liquor. When the fish are cold, drain them on slightly damp kitchen paper.

Put the egg yolks into a bowl with the mustard, salt, black pepper, sugar and herbs. Mix them well together and then add the softened butter a little at a time, stirring continuously. When all the butter has been added, adjust the consistency to that of a fairly thick mayonnaise by adding the vinegar. Place in a piping bag with a small rosette nozzle.

Arrange the mackerel fillets around the edge of a serving dish and pipe a rope design of butter along each fillet or if preferred, the butter may be served in the centre of the dish. Garnish with the parsley and serve very cold.

INGREDIENTS

To Serve 8

4 mackerel, cleaned and filleted

600ml/1pt Court bouillon (see page 67)

2 egg yolks

1 tbsp Dijon mustard

salt

black pepper

a pinch of sugar

3 tbsp chopped fresh herbs

50g/2oz softened butter

1-2 tsp white wine vinegar

sprigs of fresh parsley

Tartelettes au Roquefort

SMALL PASTRY CASES WITH A BLUE CHEESE FILLING

(Languedoc and the Centre)

Roll out the Pâte brisée on a lightly floured board and line into greased tartelette (or bun) tins. Prick well and bake blind for 15 minutes, then remove the paper and beans from the tartelettes and cook for a further 5 minutes to dry out. Increase the temperature to 220°C/425°F/Gas Mark 7.

Melt the butter in a pan and soften the onion. Remove from the heat, stir in the flour and cook for 2-3 minutes. Remove from the heat and add the milk, a little at a time. Bring to the boil, stirring continuously, and simmer for 2-3 minutes. Remove from the heat, stir in the egg yolk, Madeira, cheese, salt and black pepper to taste. Whisk the egg white until stiff and fold into the mixture.

Place 1 teaspoon of this mixture in each pastry case and bake for 20 minutes or until golden brown. Serve at once garnished with a slice of stuffed olive.

INGREDIENTS

To Serve 5-6

Pâte brisée made with 100g/4oz plain flour (see page 71)

25g/1oz butter

1 tsp grated onion

25g/1oz flour

150ml/¼pt milk

1 egg, separated

1 tbsp Madeira

75g/3oz Roquefort cheese, softened

salt

black pepper

4 stuffed olives

Pre-heat the oven to 200°C/400°F/Gas Mark 6

MAIN COURSE

The main course should be substantial enough to satisfy the appetite but not so heavy that guests feel uncomfortably full after eating it. It may be of meat, poultry, game or offal, and sometimes fish or shellfish are served. Slightly more unusual, but just as acceptable, would be a farinaceous dish or one based on eggs. The chosen dish may be complete in itself or it may need the addition of extra vegetables.

Poulet Sauté à la Provençale, chicken in a tomato sauce with bacon and thyme; recipe page 103.

Blanquette d'Agneau des Bords du Rhone

LAMB WITH VEGETABLES IN A CREAMY SAUCE
(Lyonnais)

INGREDIENTS

To Serve 4

1.5kg/3½lb shoulder of lamb

75g/3oz dripping

2 medium onions, finely chopped

2 carrots, sliced

salt

black pepper

bouquet garni

100g/4oz Beurre manié, approx. (see page 65)

150ml/¼pt Sauce mayonnaise (see page 66)

juice of 1 lemon

For the garnish

225g/8oz French beans*

225g/8oz young carrots*

1 cauliflower, cut into florets*

parsley, finely chopped

*cooked separately and tossed in butter

• *Illustration, page 117*

Remove the meat from the bone, trimming away excess fat, and cut the meat into 5cm/2 inch cubes. Heat the dripping in a pan, add the onions and carrots and cook, stirring all the time, for 5 minutes. They must not brown. Add the meat and seal in the fat, but do not let it brown. Pour in enough hot water to cover the meat, add the salt, black pepper and the bouquet garni, place the lid on the pan and simmer gently for 45-60 minutes or until tender.

Add the Beurre manié a little at a time over the heat until a fairly thin sauce is obtained and the flour is cooked.

Remove the meat and vegetables with a draining spoon and place the meat in a hot serving dish. Discard the bouquet garni. Mix a little of the liquor with the Sauce mayonnaise, return to the pan, mix well, add the lemon juice, taste and adjust the seasoning. Strain the sauce over the meat, garnish with the vegetables and sprinkle with the parsley. Serve at once.

Pintade Chasseur

GUINEA FOWL WITH WINE AND MUSHROOMS
(Franche-Comté)

INGREDIENTS

To Serve 4

40g/1½oz butter

1 tbsp oil

1.25kg/2½lb guinea fowl

½ onion, finely chopped

1 tsp tomato purée

150ml/¼pt dry white wine

300ml/½pt white stock (see page 68)

1 clove of garlic, crushed

salt

black pepper

100g/4oz mushrooms, sliced

parsley, chopped

Heat the butter and oil in a thick pan and brown the guinea fowl on all sides. Remove it and add the onion, tomato purée, wine, stock and the garlic. Bring to simmering point and return the guinea fowl to the pan. Season with salt and black pepper, cover with greaseproof paper and a lid, and simmer for 30-40 minutes.

Add the mushrooms and cook for 10 minutes, taste and adjust the seasoning. Place the guinea fowl on a hot serving dish, pour over the gravy and sprinkle with the parsley. Serve hot.

POULET SAUTE A LA PROVENCALE

CHICKEN IN A TOMATO SAUCE WITH BACON AND THYME

(Provence)

Place a sprig of thyme on each chicken joint, wrap a rasher of bacon around each, and secure with string.

Heat the butter and oil in a thick pan and fry the chicken joints until they are a good rich brown. Remove the chicken joints, add the onion and tomatoes and cook until tender. Pour off the surplus fat, sprinkle in the flour and mix well. Pour on the wine, add the garlic, salt and black pepper, and bring to the boil. Replace the chicken, cover and simmer gently for 45-60 minutes or until tender.

Remove the string from the chicken joints and place them in a hot serving dish. Reduce the liquor in which the chicken has been cooked until it is the consistency of thin cream, taste and adjust the seasoning, and pour over the chicken. Garnish with the French bread and sprinkle with the parsley.

INGREDIENTS

To Serve 4-6

8 sprigs of thyme

1.5-1.75kg/3½-4lb chicken, jointed

8 rashers of back bacon

50g/2oz butter

5-6 tbsp oil

1 large onion, chopped

4 tomatoes, skinned, pipped and cut into shreds

1 tsp flour

300ml/½pt dry white wine

1 clove of garlic, crushed

salt

black pepper

8 slices of French bread fried in oil

parsley, finely chopped

• *Illustration, page 100. See page 46 for step-by-step illustrations of jointing a chicken.*

ROTI DE PORC A L'AIL

GARLIC FLAVOURED ROAST PORK

(Languedoc and the Centre)

The meat should be prepared 12 hours in advance. Peel the garlic, cut into strips, and insert the strips under the rind and in the flesh of the pork. Season with salt and black pepper and sprinkle with the oil.

Place the pork in a roasting pan with the whole carrot and onion and cook for 2¼ hours. Place on a hot serving dish.

Strain off the fat from the pan, retaining the juices, then add the flour, replace over the heat, and brown well. Add the stock slowly, mixing in all the residue from the sides of the pan, and bring to the boil. Taste, adjust the seasoning and strain. Serve this sauce separately.

♦ If you wish to vary the size of the meat, allow 30 minutes per 450g/ 1lb plus 30 minutes extra.

INGREDIENTS

To Serve 6

2 cloves of garlic

1.5kg/3½lb loin or leg of pork

salt

black pepper

2 tbsp oil

1 carrot

1 onion

1 tsp flour

300ml/½pt white stock (see page 68)

Pre-heat the oven to 200°C/ 400°F/Gas Mark 6

• *Illustration, page 104*

Rôti de Porc à l'Ail, garlic flavoured roast pork served with a simple gravy; recipe page 103.

FAISAN A LA VALLEE D'AUGE

PHEASANT COOKED WITH CIDER AND APPLES IN A CREAM SAUCE

(Normandy)

In the Auge valley, home of the finest Calvados, the grass is said to grow so fast that a stick left lying out at night is covered by the morning.

INGREDIENTS

To Serve 2-4

75g/3oz butter

1 pheasant, trussed

2 cooking apples, peeled, cored and sliced

salt

black pepper

1 level tbsp flour

300ml/½pt draught cider

bouquet garni

2 eating apples, peeled, cored and sliced in rings

150ml/¼pt double cream

parsley, finely chopped

4-6 tbsp 5mm/¼ inch croûtons (see page 52)

Pre-heat the oven to 160°C/325°F/Gas Mark 3.

● *Illustration, page 120. See page 47 for step-by-step illustrations of trussing.*

Melt half the butter in a deep pan and brown the pheasant quickly on all sides. Remove the pheasant from the pan and add the cooking apples, salt and black pepper and cook gently for 5 minutes, stirring continuously. Add the flour and allow to brown, stirring occasionally. Pour in the cider, bring slowly to the boil, replace the pheasant and add the bouquet garni. Taste and adjust the seasoning. Cover with greaseproof paper and the lid and cook for 1 hour or until tender.

Melt the remaining butter in a frying pan and cook the eating apples, allowing them to brown slightly. Keep warm.

Put the pheasant on a hot serving dish and keep warm. Bring the cooking liquor to the boil and cook rapidly for 5 minutes. Discard the bouquet garni. Add the cream, reheat, taste and adjust the seasoning. Pour the sauce over the pheasant and sprinkle with the parsley. Garnish with the croûtons and apple rings.

◊ If the pheasant tail feathers are available, they may be used as a garnish.

MULET A LA PROVENCALE

GREY MULLET WITH TOMATOES AND ONIONS

(Provence)

INGREDIENTS

To Serve 4

2 tbsp oil

2 onions, chopped

450g/1lb tomatoes, skinned and chopped

2 cloves of garlic, crushed

4 tbsp dry white wine

salt

black pepper

750g/1½lb grey mullet, cleaned and scaled

parsley, finely chopped

Heat the oil in a pan and cook the onion lightly. Add the tomatoes, garlic, wine, salt and black pepper and simmer gently for 10 minutes.

Remove the head, tail and fins from the fish, cut the fish into 5cm/2 inch slices and place in the tomato mixture. Cover and cook slowly for 20 minutes.

Place the fish on a warm serving dish. Add 1 teaspoon of chopped parsley to the sauce, taste and adjust the seasoning, pour over the fish and sprinkle with a little more parsley. Serve hot.

LOTTE A L'ARMORICAINE

MONKFISH WITH A SPICY TOMATO SAUCE

(Brittany)

Armorica is the ancient name for Brittany. Monkfish is known as 'poor man's lobster' because of its resilient texture.

Remove the transparent skin from the fish, cut the flesh into fillets or steaks, and coat with the seasoned flour. Heat the oil and butter in a frying pan and cook the fish quickly until set and lightly coloured.

Remove the fish from the pan, and add the carrot, shallots, onion and garlic. Cover and cook gently over a low heat for 5 minutes. Add the bouquet garni, tarragon, tomato purée, saffron, cayenne pepper, curry powder, salt and black pepper and stir in the white wine and brandy.

Return the fish to the pan and simmer gently, uncovered, for 45 minutes or until tender. Add the cream, taste and adjust the seasoning. Serve hot.

INGREDIENTS

To Serve 4

750g/1½lb monkfish
3-4 tbsp seasoned flour
2 tbsp oil
25g/1 oz butter
1 carrot, grated
2 shallots, finely chopped
1 onion, finely chopped
1 clove of garlic, crushed
bouquet garni
a sprig of tarragon
3-4 tbsp tomato purée
a pinch of powdered saffron
a pinch of cayenne pepper
a pinch of curry powder
salt
black pepper
300ml/½pt dry white wine
1 tbsp brandy
1-2 tbsps double cream

RAIE AU BEURRE NOIR

SKATE WITH BLACK BUTTER

(Brittany)

Wash the fish and cut into even sized portions. Place the fish in the Court bouillon and simmer gently for 15-20 minutes. Drain well and scrape off the skin on each side. Place on a serving dish and keep hot.

Heat the butter in a frying pan until it turns a deep brown colour. Season with salt and black pepper and pour it over the fish. Add the vinegar to the pan, and heat well, allowing it to reduce by half. Pour this over the fish, and sprinkle over the capers and the parsley. Serve at once.

INGREDIENTS

To Serve 4

1kg/2lb skate
600ml/1pt Court bouillon (see page 67)
75-100g/3-4oz butter
salt
black pepper
2-3 tbsp wine vinegar
2 tbsp capers
1 tbsp finely chopped parsley

• *Illustration, page 108*

Raie au Beurre Noir, a delicious and simple to prepare fish dish of skate with black butter; recipe page 107.

F ILET DE SOLE ILE DE FRANCE

SOLE WITH BERCY SAUCE, MUSHROOMS, TOMATOES AND ASPARAGUS

(Ile de France and the North)

To Serve 4

8 fillets of sole

1 slice of carrot

1 slice of onion

$\frac{1}{2}$ bayleaf

salt

3-4 peppercorns

150ml/$\frac{1}{4}$pt white wine or dry cider

150ml/$\frac{1}{4}$pt water

50g/2oz mushrooms, sliced

65g/2$\frac{1}{2}$oz butter

$\frac{1}{2}$ tsp lemon juice

225g/8oz tomatoes, skinned, pipped and cut into shreds

175g/6oz cooked asparagus tips

Sauce Bercy

15g/$\frac{1}{2}$oz butter

1 tbsp finely chopped shallots

300ml/$\frac{1}{2}$pt white wine or dry cider

salt

black pepper

parsley, chopped

$\frac{1}{2}$ tsp lemon juice

50g/2oz Beurre manié, approx. (see page 65)

Pre-heat the oven to 180°C/ 350°F/Gas Mark 4

• *Illustration, page 132. See page 39 for step-by-step illustrations of preparing sole*

Skin the fish fillets and fold each one in half with the skin side inside. Place the fillets in a shallow fireproof dish with the carrot, onion, bayleaf, salt and peppercorns. Pour over the wine and water, cover with buttered greaseproof paper and poach in the oven for 15-20 minutes.

For the sauce, melt the butter in a small pan and cook the shallots until soft but not brown. Add the wine or cider, reduce by half quickly over a good heat, then pour in 150ml/$\frac{1}{4}$pt of the liquor in which the fish was poached. Season with salt, black pepper, parsley and lemon juice. Add the Beurre manié to the sauce a little at a time and whisk over the heat until the sauce thickens and the flour is cooked.

Arrange the fish in a fireproof dish, pour over the Sauce Bercy and brown under a hot grill.

Cook the mushrooms in 25g/1oz of the butter and the lemon juice until tender and drain well. Heat the tomatoes and asparagus separately in the remaining butter and drain well. Garnish the fish with the mushrooms, tomatoes and asparagus.

ROGNONS D'AGNEAU A LA BEAUJOLAISE

KIDNEYS IN A WINE AND MUSTARD SAUCE

(Burgundy)

Cut the kidneys in half and remove the cores.

Melt the butter in a pan, add the onion and cook until it is soft and transparent. Add the kidneys, fry until tender and place on a warm serving dish.

Pour the wine into the pan, bring to the boil and reduce by half. Mix the cream and mustard together, add to the wine and heat through without boiling. Season with salt and black pepper, pour over the kidneys, sprinkle with parsley and serve at once.

♦ The kidneys are cooked when no blood runs from them when tested with the point of a knife. If overcooked, they will become dry and rubbery.

INGREDIENTS

To Serve 2-4

8 lamb's kidneys, skinned
50g/2oz butter
1 onion, chopped
150ml/¼pt Beaujolais
2 tbsp double cream
1 tbsp French mustard
salt
black pepper
parsley, chopped

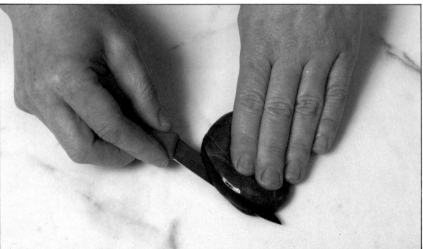

Preparing the kidneys. Holding the kidney firmly against a cutting surface, cut through the round side towards the centre, but keep the halves joined.

Using kitchen scissors, snip around the core in the centre of the kidney and remove it.

Caille à la Vigneronne,
quail in a wine sauce and
garnished with fresh
grapes; recipe page 115.

GELINE DE TOURAINE EN FRICASSEE VOUVRIONNE

CHICKEN WITH A VOUVRAY AND CREAM SAUCE
(Anjou and the Loire)

In the seventeenth century, the Sarthe area north of the Loire was famous for its chickens fed on aniseed and musk. Today Lové in the same district produces chickens with a special red label which are claimed to rival those of Bresse.

INGREDIENTS

To Serve 4

50g/2oz butter

1.5kg/3½lb chicken, jointed

12 small pickling onions, peeled

2 tbsp flour

150ml/¼pt dry Vouvray

300ml/½pt water

salt

black pepper

1 small clove of garlic, crushed

bouquet garni

3 sprigs of tarragon

100g/4oz button mushrooms, quartered

3 egg yolks

3 tbsp double cream

2 tbsp brandy

Pre-heat the oven to 190°C/ 375°F/Gas Mark 5

• *See page 46 for step-by-step illustrations of jointing a chicken*

Heat the butter in a large pan, add the chicken joints, and turn them in the hot butter until they are sealed. Do not allow them to brown. Remove the chicken joints and add the small onions to the pan. Cover with a lid and shake them over a gentle heat until the onions are tender. Sprinkle in the flour and stir, allowing it to colour slightly, then pour in the wine and the water. Add the salt, black pepper, garlic, bouquet garni and tarragon and bring to the boil.

Replace the chicken joints, add the mushrooms, cover with the lid and simmer for 45-60 minutes. Arrange the chicken joints on a warm serving dish and keep hot. Remove the bouquet garni.

Whisk the egg yolks with the cream and brandy, pour a little of the hot liquor in which the chicken was cooked into the cream and brandy, and mix well. Return to the pan and thicken over a low heat without allowing it to boil. Taste and adjust the seasoning. Arrange the onions and mushrooms at each end of the dish, strain the sauce over the chicken and serve at once.

♦ If allowed to boil, the sauce will curdle.

CAILLE A LA VIGNERONNE

QUAIL IN A WINE SAUCE WITH GRAPES

(Burgundy)

Heat the butter in a pan and brown the quail quickly on all sides. Remove from the pan, add the vegetables and cook for 7-10 minutes or until lightly coloured. Pour off any excess fat and place the quail on top of the vegetables. Flame the quail with the warmed brandy, and add the wine, stock, bouquet garni, salt and black pepper. Cover with a lid and cook for 15-20 minutes.

Remove the quail from the pan and keep hot. Strain the cooking liquor into a clean pan, and heat the grapes through. Remove and keep hot. Allow the liquor to reduce by at least half so that it is thick and syrupy. Taste and adjust the seasoning.

Remove the trussing strings and place the quail on the croûtes. Immediately before serving, pour the sauce over the top of each bird, sprinkle with the parsley and garnish the dish with the grapes.

INGREDIENTS

To Serve 2-4

50g/2oz butter

4 quail, trussed

1 small onion, chopped

1 carrot, chopped

1 leek, chopped

2 sticks of celery, chopped

2 tbsp brandy

300ml/½pt white wine

300ml/½pt white stock (see page 68)

bouquet garni

salt

black pepper

100g/4oz black grapes, pipped

100g/4oz white grapes, pipped

4 oval croûtes 7.5cm/3 inches in diameter (see page 52)

parsley, finely chopped

Pre-heat the oven to 190°C/ 375°F/Gas Mark 5

• *Illustration, page 112. See page 47 for step-by-step illustrations of trussing.*

POULET PERIGOURDINE

CHICKEN WITH TRUFFLES

(Pays Basque)

Place the chicken in a roasting pan, season with salt and black pepper, and spread with butter. Add the carrot and onion, cover with tin foil and cook for 1 hour or until tender. Remove the foil 20 minutes before the end of the cooking time to allow the chicken to brown.

Remove the chicken from the roasting pan and cut into joints. Pour off the surplus fat from the roasting pan and déglace the pan with the Sauce demi-glace. Strain into a clean pan, add the chicken joints and truffles and heat gently together for 15 minutes. Taste and adjust the seasoning and the consistency.

Arrange the chicken joints on a hot serving dish and pour the sauce over.

INGREDIENTS

To Serve 4-6

1.5kg/3½lb chicken, trussed

salt

black pepper

50g/2oz butter

1 carrot

1 onion

300ml/½pt Sauce demi-glace (see page 65)

2 truffles, chopped

Pre-heat the oven to 200°C/ 400°F/Gas Mark 6

• *See page 47 for step-by-step illustrations of trussing.*

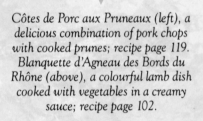

Côtes de Porc aux Pruneaux (left), a
delicious combination of pork chops
with cooked prunes; recipe page 119.
Blanquette d'Agneau des Bords du
Rhône (above), a colourful lamb dish
cooked with vegetables in a creamy
sauce; recipe page 102.

Omelette Lyonnaise aux Croutons

ONION OMELETTE WITH CROUTONS

(Lyonnais)

INGREDIENTS

To Serve 2-3

50g/2oz butter

2 medium onions, thinly sliced

6 eggs

salt

black pepper

4-6 tbsp 5mm/¼ inch croûtons (see page 52)

½ tsp wine vinegar

Heat three-quarters of the butter in a frying pan and fry the onions until they are soft and golden brown. Remove from the pan and keep hot.

Beat the eggs, add the salt and black pepper, and pour into the hot pan. Tilt the pan so the eggs run smoothly over the surface and with a fork draw the mixture from the sides towards the centre like the spokes of a wheel. Lift the edges of the omelette and allow the liquid egg to run underneath.

Cover the surface of the omelette with the onions and croûtons, fold the omelette in half and tip onto a hot plate. Melt the remaining butter in the pan, brown it slightly, then stir in the vinegar and pour over the omelette.

Cassoulet

CASSEROLE OF HARICOT BEANS WITH A SELECTION OF MEATS

(Languedoc and the Centre)

INGREDIENTS

To Serve 4-6

450g/1lb haricot beans, soaked overnight

450g/1lb blade of pork, boneless

100g/4oz green bacon

225g/8oz garlic-flavoured boiling sausage

1 onion

bouquet garni

1 clove of garlic

salt

black pepper

350g/12oz breast or shoulder of lamb, boneless

100g/4oz breadcrumbs

Pre-heat the oven to 200°C/ 400°F/Gas Mark 6.

Remove the rind from the pork and bacon and cut it into small squares. Place this in a large pan with the piece of bacon, haricot beans, whole boiling sausage, onion, bouquet garni, garlic, salt and black pepper. Cover with water and simmer for 2 hours.

Place the pork and lamb in a roasting pan and cook for 30 minutes. Remove the meat and reduce the temperature to 160°C/325°F/Gas Mark 3.

Drain the beans, reserving the liquid, and discard the onion, bouquet garni and the clove of garlic.

Put a layer of beans together with the pork and bacon rind in a deep fireproof dish, and cover with the boiling sausage, lamb, bacon and pork, all cut into 2.5cm/1 inch pieces. Cover with the rest of the beans, pour over 600ml/1pt of the reserved liquid, and spread a layer of breadcrumbs on the top.

Cook for 2-2½ hours or until the breadcrumbs are golden brown and the beans are moist and creamy. A little more liquid may be added during the cooking if the beans begin to look dry.

Cotes de Porc aux Pruneaux

PORK CHOPS WITH PRUNES

(Anjou and the Loire)

Simmer the prunes gently in the wine for 8-10 minutes or until tender.

Coat the chops with the seasoned flour, heat the butter in a frying pan and cook the chops, allowing 7-10 minutes on each side. Season with salt and black pepper. Place them on a warm serving dish and arrange the prunes down each side.

Pour off all but 2 tablespoons of the fat in the frying pan, add the wine from the prunes and reduce the liquor quickly over a good heat to half its quantity. Stir in the redcurrant jelly, mix well, add the cream, then taste and adjust the seasoning. Pour the sauce over the chops and serve very hot.

♦ To test when the chops are cooked, check that no red line is visible down the side of the bone and no blood is seeping from the chine bone.

INGREDIENTS

To Serve 4

16-20 prunes, soaked overnight in 300ml/½pt dry Vouvray

4 pork chops, trimmed

2 tbsp seasoned flour

50g/2oz butter

salt

black pepper

1 dsp redcurrant jelly

2 tbsp double cream

• *Illustration, page 116*

Trimming the pork chops. Remove the rind by cutting along the natural line in the fat.

119

Faisan à la Vallée d'Auge, pheasant cooked with cider and apples in a cream sauce and garnished with croûtons and apple rings; recipe page 106.

POULE AU POT FARCI A LA LORRAINE

A POACHED AND STUFFED CHICKEN WITH VEGETABLES IN A CREAMY SAUCE

(Alsace and Lorraine)

The recipe supposedly originated from the king's wish that every family in the land should have a chicken in the pot each Sunday.

INGREDIENTS

To Serve 6

1.5-1.75kg/3½-4lb chicken

450g/1lb carrots, quartered

275g/10oz turnips, quartered

4 small leeks, cleaned

For the stock

1.5lt/2½pt water

1 onion stuck with 2 cloves

1 stick of celery

bouquet garni

giblets from the chicken, excluding the liver (keep for the stuffing)

8 peppercorns

2 level tsp salt

For the stuffing

100g/4oz breadcrumbs soaked in 4 tbsp milk

100g/4oz veal, minced

100g/4oz lean bacon, minced

100g/4oz sausagemeat

chicken liver, chopped

2 cloves of garlic, crushed

2 tsp finely chopped parsley

a sprig of thyme, chopped

a pinch of nutmeg

salt

black pepper

1 egg, beaten

For the sauce

40g/1½oz butter

40g/1½oz flour

juice of ½ lemon

2 egg yolks

3 tbsp double cream

Make the stock first. Put the water in a large pan with the onion, celery, bouquet garni, giblets, peppercorns and salt. Bring to the boil, skim and allow to simmer gently while making the stuffing and preparing the chicken.

To make the stuffing, squeeze the milk out of the breadcrumbs and mix them with the rest of the ingredients. Blend very thoroughly and stuff the body and under the breast skin of the chicken with this mixture. Truss the chicken, place in the pan of stock — adding more water if required to nearly cover the bird — and simmer very gently with a lid on the pan for 1 hour. Add the carrots, turnips and leeks and cook for a further hour or until the chicken and vegetables are tender.

Remove 1lt/1¾pt of the stock and reduce by half in a clean pan. Melt the butter for the sauce in a small pan, remove from the heat, stir in the flour and cook for 2-3 minutes. Remove from the heat, add the reduced stock and lemon juice, bring to the boil stirring all the time, and cook for 4-5 minutes.

Drain the chicken and vegetables (discarding the stock vegetables) and arrange on a warm serving dish.

Whisk the egg yolks with the cream, pour a little of the hot sauce onto the egg yolk and cream mixture, then return to the pan. Thicken over a low heat without allowing it to boil. Taste and adjust the seasoning, strain the sauce, pour some over the meat and vegetables and serve the rest in a sauce boat.

♦ If the sauce is allowed to boil with the egg and cream mixture in, it will curdle.

CHOUCROUTE GARNI

SAUERKRAUT WITH PORK AND FRANKFURTER SAUSAGES

(Alsace and Lorraine)

Melt the dripping in a heavy pan, add the onion and cook until starting to colour. Add the sauerkraut, white wine, apple and juniper berries and cook for 5 minutes. Stir in the stock, cover and cook for 1 hour.

Add the belly of pork and cook for a further hour, then add the garlic sausage and cook for half an hour.

Simmer the frankfurter sausages in a pan of water for 10 minutes, drain and arrange on top of the sauerkraut.

INGREDIENTS
To Serve 4
2 tbsp dripping
1 onion, chopped
1 can of sauerkraut
150ml/¼pt white wine
1 cooking apple, peeled, cored and chopped
12 juniper berries
600ml/1pt white stock (see page 68)
450g/1lb belly of pork, sliced
100g/4oz garlic sausage, sliced
4 frankfurter sausages

CARBONNADE DE BOEUF FLAMANDE

BEEF COOKED IN BEER

(Ile de France and the North)

'Carbonnade' comes from 'charbon', or coals, as the meat was once grilled rather than stewed.

Melt the butter in a thick pan and cook the onions and sugar until well browned. Remove the onions from the pan.

Cut the meat into 5cm/2 inch cubes, coat with seasoned flour and brown in the hot fat. Return the onions to the pan, add the garlic, beer, salt and black pepper and cover tightly with greaseproof paper and a lid. Cook for 2-2½ hours or until the meat is tender.

Remove the meat from the pan with a draining spoon, place in a serving dish and keep warm. Reduce the liquor to the consistency of thin cream, taste and adjust the seasoning, and pour over the meat.

INGREDIENTS
To Serve 4-6
50g/2oz butter
750g/1½lb onions, thinly sliced
1 level tbsp brown sugar
750g/1½lb chuck steak
1 tbsp seasoned flour
1 clove of garlic, crushed
600ml/1pt beer
salt
black pepper
Pre-heat the oven to 180°C/ 350°F/Gas Mark 4.

Truites Grenobloise, trout
stuffed with capers and
garnished with slices of
lemon; recipe page 127.

125

BOEUF EN DAUBE PROVENCALE

INGREDIENTS

To Serve 6-8

1.5kg/3¼lb chuck steak

225g/8oz fat bacon, cut into lardons

1 onion, quartered

4-5 cloves of garlic

bouquet garni

7.5cm/3 inch piece of orange rind

450ml/¾pt hot water

For the marinade

2 onions, quartered

2 carrots, quartered

bouquet garni

½ tsp mixed spice

salt

black pepper

600ml/1pt red wine

150ml/¼pt wine vinegar

Pre-heat the oven to 180°C/ 350°F/Gas Mark 4

AN AROMATIC BEEF STEW

(Provence)

Cut the beef into 75g/3oz pieces. Put them in a shallow dish with the marinade ingredients, and allow to marinate for 8-9 hours or overnight.

Fry the bacon until the fat runs from it, remove the bacon, then add the onion and brown it in the bacon fat. Add the well drained beef and vegetables, and fry until brown. Pour in the wine from the marinade, and add the garlic, bouquet garni, orange rind and bacon. Leave uncovered and simmer until the liquid content has reduced by half.

Pour on the hot water, taste and adjust the seasoning, cover the pan with tin foil and a lid and cook for 4-5 hours. Take out the bouquet garni and orange rind and remove the excess grease before serving.

TRIPES A LA MODE DE CAEN

INGREDIENTS

To Serve 4-6

1.25kg/2½lb fresh tripe

2 calf's feet

2 tbsp oil

450g/1lb onions, sliced

350g/12oz carrots, sliced

1 clove of garlic, crushed

bouquet garni

salt

150ml/¼pt dry cider or white wine

25ml/1fl oz Calvados

white pepper

Pre-heat the oven to 180°C/ 350°F/Gas Mark 4.

TRIPE WITH VEGETABLES AND CALVADOS

(Normandy)

This was probably perfected, if not actually invented, by a fourteenth-century chef named Benoit, a native of Caen. After eating your tripe, it may be sensible to follow the Norman custom of drinking a 'trou Normand' or glass of Calvados as a digestive before going on to the next course,.

Wash the tripe in cold water and cut into 5cm/2 inch squares. Blanch the tripe and calf's feet in boiling water for 5 minutes.. Drain and rinse.

Heat the oil in a large pan, add the onions, carrots and garlic, and cook slowly, stirring occasionally, until soft but not brown. Add the tripe, calf's feet, bouquet garni, salt and water to cover. Bring to the boil, cover and cook stirring occasionally for 6 hours or until very tender. About 15 minutes before serving, stir in the cider or wine, Calvados and white pepper, bring back to the boil and simmer uncovered until the gravy is shiny. Taste and adjust the seasoning. Remove the bouquet garni and serve in deep bowls.

Truites Grenobloise

STUFFED TROUT WITH CAPERS

(Franche-Comté)

Remove the backbone from the trout. Mix the breadcrumbs with the herbs, 15g/½ oz melted butter, salt and black pepper and add sufficient egg to bind together.

Stuff the fish with this mixture and coat them with seasoned flour. Melt the remaining butter in a frying pan and fry the fish until golden brown on each side and cooked through. Place on a warm serving dish and keep hot.

Déglace the pan with the juice of 1 lemon, stir in the capers and pour over the fish. Remove the skin and pith from the second lemon, cut the flesh into thin slices and garnish the fish with this. Sprinkle with the parsley.

INGREDIENTS

To Serve 4

4 trout, cleaned

2 tbsp fresh white breadcrumbs

1 tbsp finely chopped fresh herbs

100g/4oz butter

salt

black pepper

a little beaten egg

seasoned flour

2 lemons

2 tbsp capers

parsley, chopped

● *Illustration, page 124. See page 38 for step-by-step illustrations of cleaning trout*

Oie aux Cerises

ROAST GOOSE WITH CHERRIES AND APPLES

(Pays Basque and the South-West)

Spread about half the butter over the goose and sprinkle with salt and black pepper. Place the goose on its side on a rack in a deep roasting pan and cover with tin foil. Cook for 25 minutes, turn the goose over and cook for a further 25 minutes. Reduce the temperature to 160°C/ 325°F/Gas Mark 3, remove the tin foil, turn the goose onto its back, baste well and cook for a further 1½ hours or until tender.

Peel the apples and remove as much of the centre as possible without damaging the apple. Put them in another roasting pan, brush with melted butter and place a lump of sugar in the centre of each. Cook on the shelf below the goose until tender — about 15 minutes.

Remove the goose from the oven and drain the fat that has collected inside the bird. Keep the goose hot. Pour off the excess fat from the roasting pan. Heat the cherries in the wine, then strain and déglace the roasting pan with the wine. Taste and adjust the seasoning.

Place the goose on a warm serving dish, arrange the apples all around with the cherries in between them putting 1 or 2 cherries on the top of each apple. Sprinkle with the parsley and serve the gravy separately.

INGREDIENTS

To Serve 6

50g/2oz butter

2.75kg/7lb goose, trussed

salt

black pepper

12 even-sized dessert apples

12 lumps of sugar

1kg/2lb red cherries, stoned and cooked with 50g/2oz sugar

300ml/½pt red wine

parsley, chopped

Pre-heat the oven to 200°C/ 400°F/Gas Mark 6.

● *See page 47 for step-by-step illustrations of trussing*

Gigot aux Haricots à la Bretonne, roast leg of lamb with haricot beans; recipe page 131.

Coq au vin

CHICKEN IN RED WINE
(Burgundy)

INGREDIENTS

INGREDIENTS

To Serve 4-6

1 tbsp oil

40g/1½oz butter

75g/3oz lean bacon, cut into lardons

350g/12oz small pickling onions, peeled

1.5kg/3½lb chicken, jointed

3 tbsp brandy

1 tbsp flour

600ml/1pt red wine

bouquet garni

a sprig of rosemary

1 tbsp sugar

a pinch of nutmeg

175g/6oz button mushrooms

salt

black pepper

heart shaped croûtons (see page 52)

Pre-heat the oven to 180°C/350°F/Gas Mark 4.

● *See page 46 for step-by-step illustrations of jointing a chicken*

Heat the oil and butter in a heavy pan and cook the bacon and onions until they are golden brown. Remove them and brown the chicken joints in the pan and flame with the warmed brandy. Remove the chicken joints. Sprinkle in the flour and cook for 2-3 minutes, stirring well.

Return the chicken joints, onions and bacon to the pan, pour in the wine and add the bouquet garni, rosemary, sugar, nutmeg, mushrooms, salt and black pepper. Cover with greaseproof paper and a lid and cook for approximately 1 hour or until the chicken is tender.

Arrange the chicken joints on a hot serving dish, placing the mushrooms at each end of the dish and the onions along the sides. Remove the grease from the pan, re-heat, taste and adjust the seasoning and strain the liquor over the chicken joints. Garnish with the croûtons.

Boeuf a la bourguignonne

BEEF IN RED WINE WITH ONIONS AND MUSHROOMS
(Burgundy)

INGREDIENTS

To Serve 4-6

750g/1½lb chuck steak

1 tbsp dripping

1 tbsp flour

150ml/¼pt red wine

150ml/¼pt water

1 clove of garlic, crushed

1 dsp tomato purée

salt

black pepper

50g/2oz lean bacon, cut into lardons

12 small pickling onions, peeled

100g/4oz button mushrooms, quartered

parsley, finely chopped

Cut the meat into 5cm/2 inch cubes. Melt the dripping in a thick pan and brown the meat well on all sides. Sprinkle with the flour and stir until brown. Add the wine, water, garlic, tomato purée, salt and black pepper.

Fry the bacon in a clean pan until the fat runs from it, then add the onions and brown them. Add the onions and bacon to the meat, cover with greaseproof paper and a lid and cook over a very gentle heat for 2¼ hours.

Add the mushrooms and cook for a further 10-15 minutes. Remove the excess grease from the liquor, taste and adjust the seasoning. Arrange on a hot serving dish and sprinkle with the parsley.

GIGOT AUX HARICOTS A LA BRETONNE

FRENCH ROAST LEG OF LAMB WITH HARICOT BEANS
(Brittany)

Place the haricot beans in a large pan, and cover with cold water. Add the bouquet garni, carrots and onions and cook gently for 2-3 hours or until tender. Rinse and drain well. Discard the bouquet garni, carrots and onions.

Brown the bacon carefully in 25g/1oz of the dripping or lard in the bottom of a roasting pan. Remove the bacon with a draining spoon, and mix with the haricot beans, cream and the butter. Add salt and black pepper and pour this mixture into a large fireproof dish. Keep on one side.

Score a diamond pattern on the outside of the lamb and cover with the remaining dripping or lard, season and place in the fat in the roasting pan. Cook for 20 minutes then reduce the temperature to 190°C/375°F/Gas Mark 5, and continue cooking for a further 60-80 minutes. Baste from time to time with a little hot stock.

About 15 minutes before the lamb is cooked, return the haricot bean mixture to the oven to heat through. When ready to serve, place the lamb on top of the haricot bean mixture.

INGREDIENTS

To Serve 6-8

225g/8oz haricot beans, soaked in cold water overnight

bouquet garni

2 carrots

2 onions stuck with 3 or 4 cloves

225g/8oz lean bacon, cut into lardons

75g/3oz dripping or lard

150ml/¼pt single cream

75g/3oz butter

salt

black pepper

1.75kg/4lb leg of lamb

300ml/½pt white stock approx (see page 68)

Pre-heat the oven to 200°C/ 400°F/Gas Mark 6

• Illustration, page 128

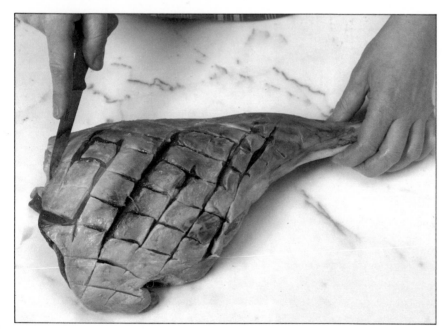

Scoring the lamb. Use a sharp kitchen knife to score the lamb joint in diamond shapes.

*Filet de Sole Ile de France,
sole served with Sauce
Bercy and garnished with
mushrooms, tomatoes
and asparagus;
recipe page 110.*

133

ESCALOPES DE VEAU ROUSSILLON

INGREDIENTS

To Serve 4

450g/1lb aubergines

salt

a little milk

5-6 tbsp seasoned flour

150ml/¼pt oil (approx.)

4 veal escalopes

50g/2oz Gruyère cheese, thinly sliced

25g/1oz Parmesan cheese, grated

25g/1oz butter

Sauce tomate

1kg/2lb fresh tomatoes, or 1 large tin of tomatoes, roughly chopped

1 onion, sliced

3 rashers of bacon, cut into lardons

1 clove of garlic, crushed

1 level tsp sugar

bouquet garni

salt

black pepper

VEAL ESCALOPES WITH AUBERGINES AND TOMATO SAUCE

(Languedoc and the Centre)

Make the sauce first. Place all the ingredients in a pan and cook over a low heat for 20 minutes or until the vegetables are tender. Sieve the sauce, taste and adjust the seasoning.

Meanwhile, cut the aubergines into 1cm/½ inch slices. Dust them lightly with salt and put on a wire rack to drain for half an hour, turning them from time to time. Dry on kitchen paper.

Dip the aubergines into milk, then into seasoned flour, and fry them quickly in the hot oil. Arrange the fried aubergines in the bottom of a fireproof dish, pour over the Sauce tomate and put aside to keep hot.

Flatten the escalopes, trim them into even shapes and dip in seasoned flour. Fry the escalopes in a little hot oil, allowing approximately 4-5 minutes on each side, depending on the thickness.

Arrange them on top of the aubergines and Sauce tomate and cover with the Gruyère cheese. Sprinkle with the Parmesan cheese, dot with knobs of the butter and place for a few moments under a hot grill. Serve at once.

♦ It is preferable when sieving the tomato sauce to use a vegetable mill in order to obtain a thick purée. Remove the bouquet garni first.

PERDREAUX A LA CATALANE

STUFFED PARTRIDGE WITH GARLIC

(Languedoc and the Centre)

Mix all the ingredients for the forcemeat together and stuff the partridge with this mixture. Truss the partridge and bard with the fat bacon. Heat the dripping in a pan and cook the partridge until golden brown. Add the ham, cook for 1 minute, then stir in the flour and cook again. Add the wine, stock, tomato purée, bouquet garni, orange rind, salt and black pepper, cover and allow to simmer for 10 minutes.

Peel the cloves of garlic, place in cold water, bring to the boil and blanch for 5 minutes. Drain and add them to the partridge.

Place in the oven and cook until tender. Remove the bouquet garni, orange rind, barding fat and trussing string. Arrange the partridge on a warm serving dish, taste the sauce, adjust the seasoning and pour over the partridge.

♦ The cooking time may be as little as 45 minutes for tender young partridges, or $2\frac{1}{2}$ hours for old ones, which do, however, become very tender when cooked in this way.

The amount of garlic may seem to be excessive but when cooked in this way it becomes palatable.

INGREDIENTS

To Serve 4

4 partridge

fat bacon

2 tbsp dripping

50g/2oz ham, diced

2 tbsp flour

85ml/3fl oz white wine

200ml/7 fl oz white stock

1 tbsp tomato purée

bouquet garni

5cm/2 inch piece of orange rind

salt

black pepper

12 cloves of garlic

For the forcemeat

100g/4oz chicken livers, chopped

50g/2oz lean ham, chopped

25g/1oz breadcrumbs

1 dsp chopped parsley

1 clove of garlic, crushed

salt

black pepper

1 egg yolk

Pre-heat the oven to 160°C/ 325°F/Gas Mark 3

VEGETABLES

In France vegetables often form a course by themselves. If they are to accompany the main course, they should not be so distinctive that they dominate the main dish, but should add colour and freshness of their own to the meal. Sometimes a salad is served in place of a vegetable or at the end of the meal to cleanse the palate.

◆

Fenouil à la Provençale, braised fennel cooked with tomatoes; recipe page 147.

Asperges a la flamande

ASPARAGUS WITH HARDBOILED EGGS
(Ile de France and the North)

INGREDIENTS

To Serve 4

450g/1lb asparagus

4 eggs

4 tbsp chopped parsley

50g/2oz butter, melted

salt

black pepper

● *Illustration, page 152*

Scrape the stalks of the asparagus and rinse in cold water. Tie in a bundle and cook gently in boiling water until tender. Drain well and arrange in a hot serving dish.

Hardboil the eggs and rub through a sieve while still hot. Mix with the parsley, melted butter, salt and black pepper and pour over the asparagus. Serve at once.

◆ This dish is equally suitable if leeks are used in place of asparagus.

Haricots a la creme

HARICOT BEANS WITH CREAM
(Pays Basque and the South-West)

INGREDIENTS

To Serve 4

225g/8oz haricot beans, soaked overnight

1 onion stuck with 1 clove

1 carrot

1 clove of garlic, crushed

1 stick of celery

a sprig of thyme

salt

black pepper

25g/1oz butter

1 tbsp double cream

Put the beans in a large pan with the onion, carrot, garlic, celery, thyme, salt and black pepper. Cover with cold water, bring to the boil and cook for 2-3 hours or until tender, adding more hot water if needed.

Remove the herbs, carrot, celery and onion, and discard, then drain the beans well and put into a warm serving dish. Add the butter and cream, taste and adjust the seasoning and serve hot.

GRATIN DAUPHINOIS

SLICED POTATOES BAKED IN EGG CUSTARD
(Franche-Comté)

Place the potatoes neatly in a buttered fireproof dish and season with salt, black pepper and the nutmeg.

Whisk the eggs and milk together, make a small space at the side of the potatoes and strain the egg and milk mixture into the dish.

Cover with the cheese and cook for 40 minutes or until tender. Serve in the dish.

♦ It is important that the slices of potato should be of uniform thickness otherwise they will cook unevenly.

If the egg and milk mixture is poured over the top of the potatoes, it will form a skin and may burn.

INGREDIENTS

To Serve 4

450g/1lb potatoes, peeled and thinly sliced

salt

black pepper

a good pinch of nutmeg

2 eggs

300ml/½pt hot milk

25g/1oz Gruyère cheese

Pre-heat the oven to 200-220°C/400-425°F/Gas Mark 6-7

SALADE AUX NOIX

GREEN SALAD WITH NUTS
(Franche-Comté)

Cut the pepper in half, discard the seeds and pith, and cut into fine shreds. Blanch in boiling salted water for 1 minute, drain and refresh in cold water.

Place the lettuce leaves, pepper and nuts in a salad bowl, add the chopped herbs to the vinaigrette and, just before serving, toss the salad in this.

INGREDIENTS

To Serve 4-6

1 green pepper

1 large round lettuce, washed and dried

25g/1oz walnuts, chopped

2 tbsp chopped fresh herbs

Sauce vinaigrette (see page 65)

● Illustration, page 145

Salade de Crevettes à la Dieppoise, mixed fish salad of shrimp and mussels, served in crisp lettuce leaves; recipe page 142.

Salade de Crevettes a la Dieppoise

A SHRIMP AND MUSSEL SALAD

(Normandy)

INGREDIENTS

To Serve 4-6

450g/1lb new potatoes

a sprig of mint

300ml/½pt Sauce mayonnaise (see page 66)

1kg/2lb mussels

1 shallot, chopped

65ml/2½fl oz dry white wine

black pepper

bouquet garni

3 dsp olive or salad oil

1 dsp vinegar

salt

100g/4oz shrimps, shelled

1 round lettuce, washed and dried

6 whole shrimps

• *Illustration, page 140*

Wash the potatoes and cook in boiling salted water with the mint until just tender. Drain and peel them and cut into neat dice. When cold mix with the mayonnaise.

Prepare the mussels. Any broken mussels must be discarded. If you have one which is open, give it a sharp tap and if it does not close, then the mussel is dead and must not be used as it could cause food poisoning.

When ready to cook the mussels, scrub them very well in several changes of cold water. Scrape off the barnacles with an old knife and also scrape off the beard of the mussel — the black threads on the flat hinge side of the shell. When you have finished cook them immediately.

Place the mussels, shallot, wine, black pepper and bouquet garni in a large strong pan, cover with a lid and shake over a good heat for 5 minutes or until all the mussels are fully opened. Drain the mussels and remove from their shells.

Mix the oil, vinegar, salt and some black pepper together and add the mussels and shrimps.

Arrange several good lettuce leaves on a dish in a flower design, place the potato salad on each lettuce leaf with the shrimps and mussels on top and garnish with the whole shrimps.

Haricots Verts a la Tourangelle

FRENCH BEANS IN A GARLIC FLAVOURED WHITE SAUCE

(Anjou and the Loire)

INGREDIENTS

To Serve 6

750g/1½lb French beans

300ml/½pt Sauce béchamel (see page 66)

1 clove of garlic, crushed

salt

black pepper

parsley, finely chopped

Prepare the beans and cook them in boiling salted water for 7-10 minutes. Drain them and mix with the Sauce béchamel and the garlic. Return to the pan, cover with greaseproof paper and a lid, and cook for a further 15-20 minutes or until the beans are tender.

Taste and adjust the seasoning. Pour into a hot serving dish and sprinkle with the parsley.

SALADE DE POISSON RAVIGOTE

WHITE FISH SALAD WITH A FLAVOURED MAYONNAISE

(Brittany)

Place the fish in a shallow pan, cover with the Court bouillon and poach over a very low heat for 10-15 minutes or until it is cooked. Remove from the heat, allow the fish to cool in the liquor, then drain well and remove the skin.

To make the sauce, mix all the ingredients for the sauce together and allow to stand for 1 hour. Taste and adjust the seasoning.

Cut the fish into portions, and arrange on a bed of lettuce on a serving dish. Cut the hardboiled eggs in half lengthways and arrange these cut side down between the pieces of fish. Coat the fish with the Sauce ravigote and arrange a lattice of anchovy fillets on the hardboiled eggs.

INGREDIENTS

To Serve 4-6

750g/1½lb cod fillet
1 litre/1¾pt Court bouillon (see page 67)
1 round lettuce
4 hardboiled eggs
8 anchovy fillets

Sauce ravigote

300ml/½pt Sauce mayonnaise (see page 66)
1 tsp lemon juice
2 tbsp double cream
1 shallot, finely chopped
2 gherkins, finely chopped
2 tsp capers, finely chopped
2 tsp finely chopped parsley
1 tsp chopped chives
black pepper

POMMES DE TERRE A LA PARISIENNE

GLAZED POTATO BALLS

(Ile de France and the North)

Wash and peel the potatoes and scoop out small balls with a Parisienne cutter. Place them in a pan of cold salted water, bring to the boil and cook for 2-3 minutes. Remove, drain and dry them on kitchen paper.

Heat the butter in a shallow pan, allow to colour slightly, then add the potatoes, salt and black pepper. Place a lid on the pan and cook the potatoes for 5 minutes, shaking the pan from time to time to prevent them from sticking.

Pour off any excess butter from the pan, add the Glace de viande, coat the potatoes with this, and sprinkle with the parsley. Serve at once.

INGREDIENTS

To Serve 4-6

750g/1½lb large potatoes
50-75g/2-3oz butter
salt
black pepper
2 tbsp Glace de viande (see page 216)
parsley, finely chopped

*Pommes de Terre Alsacienne (above), new potatoes served with
lardons of bacon and
spring onions; recipe page
154.
Salade aux Noix (top), green salad tossed with walnuts and fresh herbs;
recipe page 139.
Choufleur Normande (left), a cauliflower lightly cooked in butter, then mixed
with apple slices; recipe page 151.*

145

Pommes de Terre Saute Lyonnais

FRIED POTATOES AND ONIONS

(Lyonnais)

INGREDIENTS

To Serve 4-6

450g/1lb new potatoes

100g/4oz butter

450g/1lb onions, sliced

salt

black pepper

parsley, finely chopped

Wash the potatoes and cook in boiling salted water until just tender. Refresh in cold water, drain and peel them, and cut into thin slices. Heat half the butter in a frying pan, add the potatoes and cook, turning from time to time, until golden brown.

Heat the remaining butter in another pan and cook the onions slowly until they are a light golden colour and transparent. Mix with the potatoes and cook for 2-3 minutes. Place in a warm serving dish, season with salt and black pepper and sprinkle with the parsley.

Betteraves a L'Auvergnate

BEETROOT IN A SPICY SAUCE

(Languedoc and the Centre)

INGREDIENTS

To Serve 6-8

25g/1oz butter

100g/4oz lean bacon, cut into lardons

1 onion, finely chopped

25g/1oz flour

600ml/1pt white stock, approx. (see page 68)

salt

black pepper

1kg/2lb cooked beetroot, diced

1 dsp wine vinegar

a pinch of quatre épices

• Illustration, page 149

Heat the butter in a pan, add the bacon and cook for 1 minute. Stir in the onion and cook until soft and transparent. Remove from the heat, add the flour and cook, stirring continuously, for 4-5 minutes or until it starts to change colour. Mix in the stock, salt and black pepper, bring to the boil and simmer uncovered for 15 minutes.

Add the beetroot and vinegar to the sauce and simmer for 10-15 minutes. Add the quatre épices, taste and adjust the seasoning and serve hot.

SALADE DE FONDS D'ARTICHAUTS AUX CHAMPIGNONS

SALAD OF ARTICHOKE BOTTOMS AND MUSHROOMS

(Brittany)

Rub a mixing bowl with the cut clove of garlic, and pour in the lemon juice, salt and black pepper. Add the cream, whisking all the time. Stir in the mushrooms, mix well, cover and leave to marinate for 2 hours.

To prepare the artichokes, break the stem from each and cut the leaves all around the base, trimming as closely as you can manage without taking the heart itself. Cut the centre core of the leaves just above the heart, but leave the choke, the hairy centre core, attached — it will be removed after cooking. Rub with the lemon to prevent discoloration and cook in plenty of boiling salted water for 20-30 minutes or until tender. Drain and refresh, remove the choke with a teaspoon, and neaten by trimming off any remaining leaves. Arrange on a serving dish.

Taste the mushroom mixture, adjust the seasoning, place a spoonful in the middle of each artichoke bottom and sprinkle with the parsley.

INGREDIENTS

To Serve 4

1 clove of garlic

2 tbsp lemon juice

salt

black pepper

50ml/2fl oz double cream

100g/4oz mushrooms, thinly sliced

4 large artichokes

½ lemon

1 tbsp finely chopped parsley

• Illustration, page 149. See page 48 for step-by-step illustrations of preparing artichoke

FENOUIL A LA PROVENCALE

BRAISED FENNEL WITH TOMATOES

(Provence)

Wash the fennel and remove any discoloured outer leaves. Cut into quarters and blanch in boiling salted water for 15 minutes.

Place the onion, tomatoes, garlic, stock, salt and black pepper in a casserole, put the fennel on top, cover and cook for 1 hour or until tender. Serve hot.

INGREDIENTS

To Serve 4

2 roots of fennel

1 onion, finely chopped

350g/12oz tomatoes, skinned and quartered

1 clove of garlic, crushed

150ml/¼pt white stock (see page 68)

salt

black pepper

Pre-heat the oven to 200°C/ 400°F/Gas Mark 6

• Illustration, page 136

Carottes à la Vichy (top), glazed carrots sprinkled with parsley; recipe page 151.
Betteraves à l'Auvergnate (above), beetroot cooked in a spicy sauce;
recipe page 146.
Salade de Fonds d'Artichauts aux Champignons (left), a salad of artichoke
bottoms and mushrooms served with a creamy marinated sauce; recipe page
147.

149

Pommes de terre
A LA DIJONNAISE

INGREDIENTS

To Serve 4-6

75g/3oz butter

1kg/2lb potatoes, peeled and thinly sliced

225ml/7½fl oz hot water

salt

black pepper

1-2 tbsp finely chopped fresh herbs

25g/1oz unsalted butter, softened

65ml/2½fl oz double cream

1 tbsp Dijon mustard

POTATOES WITH HERBS, MUSTARD AND CREAM

(Burgundy)

Heat the butter in a thick pan, add the potatoes and cook, turning carefully from time to time, until lightly brown. Pour in the hot water, season with salt and black pepper, place a piece of greaseproof paper on the top, cover with a lid and cook over a low heat for a further 10 minutes.

Mix the herbs, unsalted butter, cream and mustard together, put the potatoes in a warm serving dish and place the cream mixture on top. Serve immediately.

Salsifis sautees au beurre

INGREDIENTS

To Serve 4

450g/1lb salsify, peeled

1 tsp flour

1 lt/1¾pt water

salt

juice of ½ lemon

50g/2oz butter

parsley, finely chopped

SALSIFY IN BUTTER

(Normandy)

Cut the salsify into 5cm/2 inch lengths. Mix the flour and water together, add the salt and lemon juice, strain into a pan and bring to the boil, stirring continuously. Add the salsify and cook for approximately 30-40 minutes or until tender and drain well.

Heat the butter in a pan, add the salsify, and brown lightly. Place in a hot serving dish and sprinkle with the parsley.

CHOUFLEUR NORMANDE

CAULIFLOWER WITH APPLES

(Normandy)

Divide the cauliflower into florets, cook for 7-10 minutes in boiling salted water and drain well. Cut the apples into thick slices, melt half the butter in a pan and cook the apples for about 15-20 minutes.

Melt the remaining butter in a clean pan and toss the cauliflower in this, allowing it to colour slightly. Season with salt and black pepper. Mix the cauliflower and apples together, taste and adjust the seasoning, sprinkle the lemon juice over and serve at once.

INGREDIENTS

To Serve 4

1 small cauliflower, washed

225g/8oz cooking apples, peeled and cored

100g/4oz butter

salt

black pepper

1 tsp lemon juice

• *Illustration, page 145*

CAROTTES A LA VICHY

GLAZED CARROTS

(Languedoc and the Centre)

Put the carrots, sugar, salt, black pepper and butter in a heavy pan and cover with cold water. Cook quickly without a lid until all the water has evaporated and the carrots are tender and glazed with the butter. Sprinkle with the parsley and place in a warm serving dish. Serve at once.

♦ The amount of water is important — if there is not enough the carrots will not be cooked when the water has evaporated. If there is too much, the carrots will be overcooked by the time the water has evaporated.

INGREDIENTS

To Serve 6

1kg/2lb new carrots, scraped

1 tsp sugar

salt

black pepper

50g/2oz unsalted butter

parsley, finely chopped

• *Illustration, page 148*

151

Asperges à la Flamande,
asparagus topped with a
creamy egg mixture;
recipe page 138.

Topinambours aux noix

JERUSALEM ARTICHOKES WITH WALNUTS

(Lyonnais)

INGREDIENTS

To Serve 4-6

750g/1½lb Jerusalem artichokes

1 tbsp oil

25g/1oz butter

salt

black pepper

a pinch of sugar

50g/2oz walnuts, roughly chopped

The arrival of Jerusalem or root artichokes from the New World to the court of Louis XV in France coincided with the visit of Indians from the Tupinamba tribe in Brazil. Now these artichokes are more popular around Lyon than in their native United States.

Peel the artichokes and slice thinly. Place in a pan of cold salted water, bring to the boil, cook for 5 minutes and drain well.

Heat the oil and butter in a frying pan, add the artichokes, salt, black pepper and sugar and cook, stirring occasionally, over a fairly high heat for 10 minutes. Add the walnuts and cook for 5 minutes or until the artichokes are tender and golden brown. Taste and adjust the seasoning.

Pommes de terre ALSACIENNE

NEW POTATOES WITH SPRING ONIONS AND BACON

(Alsace and Lorraine)

INGREDIENTS

To Serve 4-6

1kg/2lb new potatoes

50g/2oz butter

100g/4oz lean bacon, cut into lardons

15-20 spring onions, trimmed to 7.5cm/3 inch lengths

salt

black pepper

parsley, finely chopped

• *Illustration, page 144*

Scrape the potatoes and place in boiling salted water. Cook them for 10 minutes and drain well.

Melt the butter in a thick pan, add the bacon and spring onions and stir over a gentle heat for 3-4 minutes. Add the potatoes, season with salt and black pepper, cover with greaseproof paper and a lid, and cook slowly until tender, shaking the pan from time to time.

Place in a warm serving dish and sprinkle with plenty of parsley. Serve very hot.

Lentilles a la Lorraine

LENTILS WITH BACON AND ONIONS

(Alsace and Lorraine)

Cook the lentils in plenty of boiling salted water until tender. Drain them and reserve the liquor.

Melt the butter in a thick pan, add the bacon and cook until golden brown. Stir in the onions and cook until soft. Do not let them brown.

Add the lentils and as much liquor as is necessary to make a thin sauce, and cook for 5 minutes, stirring from time to time. Whisk in enough Beurre manié to give a thick purée, add the garlic, sugar, salt and black pepper, and serve very hot.

INGREDIENTS
To Serve 4
225g/8oz lentils, soaked overnight
50g/2oz butter
3-4 rashers of lean bacon, cut into lardons
2 large onions, finely chopped
Beurre manié (see page 65)
1 small clove of garlic, crushed
a pinch of sugar
salt
black pepper

Ratatouille a la Nicoise

MIXED VEGETABLE STEW

(Provence)

This vegetable dish from Provence probably gets its name from 'touiller', meaning to stir and crush.

Cut the courgettes and aubergines into 2.5cm/1 inch cubes. Sprinkle the aubergines with salt and leave to stand for 20 minutes, then drain and dry them on kitchen paper. Cut the pepper in half, discard the seeds and pith, and slice into thin julienne strips. Heat the oil in a heavy pan, add the onions and pepper, cover with a lid and cook slowly for 10 minutes. Do not allow them to brown.

Add the courgettes, aubergines, tomatoes, bouquet garni, thyme, garlic, salt and black pepper, cover with a lid and cook over a low heat for 30 minutes, shaking the pan from time to time. Remove the bouquet garni and thyme and taste and adjust the seasoning. Pour into a warm serving dish, sprinkle with the parsley and serve at once.

♦ In this recipe the skins are left on the courgettes and aubergines to add colour to the dish.

INGREDIENTS
To Serve 4-6
2 courgettes
2 large aubergines
1 large green pepper
4 tbsp olive oil
2 large onions, sliced
3 large tomatoes, skinned, pipped and chopped
bouquet garni
3 sprigs of thyme
3 cloves of garlic, crushed
salt
black pepper
parsley, finely chopped

155

DESSERTS

The dessert is the 'finale' to the meal, and it is the memory of this course that will remain with your guests. The dessert should form a complete contrast in texture, colour and appearance to the rest of the meal. A practice that is becoming more popular is to serve the cheese before the dessert. This allows the sweet flavour of the dessert to linger on the taste buds.

Fraises Glacées Chantilly, strawberries coated with raspberry purée, topped with Crème Chantilly and sprinkled with macaroons; recipe page 170.

156

LE PARIS-BREST

• Illustration, page 160.

A CHOUX PASTRY RING FILLED WITH COFFEE CUSTARD
(Ile de France and the North)

Put the choux pastry into a piping bag with a 2cm/$\frac{3}{4}$ inch plain nozzle and pipe a thick ring 18cm/7 inches in diameter on a lightly greased baking sheet. Brush with beaten egg, and sprinkle with the flaked almonds. Bake for 10 minutes then reduce the temperature to 190°C/375°F/Gas Mark 5, and continue cooking for a further 30-35 minutes. Cool on a wire rack.

Put the egg, egg yolk, sugar and flour into a bowl and mix well. Heat the milk with the coffee and pour onto the egg mixture. Stir well and pour into a clean pan. Bring to the boil then simmer for 3-4 minutes stirring all the time. At this stage it often appears lumpy but it will become smooth when boiled.

Pour into a bowl and cover with damp greaseproof paper to prevent a skin forming. Allow to cool.

Split the choux ring horizontally and put the base on a serving dish.

Whisk the cream stiffly and mix carefully with the coffee custard. Put the mixture into a piping bag with a large rosette nozzle and pipe the custard on the base of the ring. Cover with the other half of the ring and dust with icing sugar.

INGREDIENTS

To Serve 4-6

Pâte à choux made with 100g/4oz strong flour (see page 69)

beaten egg to glaze

25g/1oz flaked almonds

1 egg

1 egg yolk

50g/2oz sugar

25g/1oz flour

300ml/$\frac{1}{2}$pt milk

1 tbsp instant coffee powder

150ml/$\frac{1}{4}$pt double cream

icing sugar, sifted

Pre-heat the oven to 220°C/425°F/Gas Mark 7

CLAFOUTIS

A CHERRY AND KIRSCH PUDDING
(Pays Basque and the South-West)

A batter cake with black cherries, traditionally given to grape harvesters, which is a speciality of Berry.

Place the cherries in a well buttered fireproof dish, 2lt/3$\frac{1}{2}$pt in capacity, and sprinkle with the kirsch.

Put the flour, salt and sugar into a bowl and beat in the eggs one at a time. Add the egg yolks and gradually stir in the milk.

Strain the mixture over the cherries and bake for 45 minutes or until well risen and golden brown. Sprinkle with the icing sugar and serve warm.

INGREDIENTS

To Serve 6

450g/1lb cherries, stoned

3 tbsp kirsch

25g/1oz plain flour

a pinch of salt

50g/2oz caster sugar

4 eggs

2 egg yolks

600ml/1pt milk

1 tbsp icing sugar, sifted

Pre-heat the oven to 190°C/375°F/Gas Mark 5

Pain d'Epice a l'Orange

A SPICY ORANGE AND HONEY CAKE

(Burgundy)

Legend has it that in 992 an Armenian bishop named Gregory took refuge in the town of Pithivier. He made his own spiced Armenian honey cake which he gave to his visitors having first cleansed their spirits with canticles and psalms. 'As they tasted it his guests thought they were enjoying the delights of paradise.'

Grease an 18cm/7 inch cake tin with melted lard.

Warm 2 tablespoons of the milk and mix with the bicarbonate of soda. Mix the flour, sugar, aniseed, orange and lemon rinds together, and add the remaining milk and the warmed honey. Stir in the milk and bicarbonate of soda and beat well.

Pour into the tin, bake for 40 minutes then reduce the temperature to 160°C/325°F/Gas Mark 3 and bake for a further hour or until cooked. Cool on a wire rack.

♦ This cake will keep for several days and can be served with butter.

INGREDIENTS

To Serve 6-8

150ml/¼pt milk

1 tsp bicarbonate of soda

250g/9oz plain flour

65g/2½oz caster sugar

2 tsp powdered aniseed

grated rind of ½ orange

grated rind of ½ lemon

100g/4oz honey

Pre-heat the oven to 180°C/350°F/Gas Mark 4

Gateau au Chocolate de Nancy

RICH CHOCOLATE CAKE

(Alsace and Lorraine)

Grease a 16.5cm/6½ inch moule à manqué or cake tin with extra melted butter.

Melt the chocolate by standing it on a plate over a pan of hot water. Cream the butter, add the melted chocolate and the egg yolks one at a time. Fold in the sugar, vanilla sugar, flour and ground almonds.

Beat the egg whites stiffly and fold them into the chocolate mixture as quickly as possible. Pour into the tin — it should only be three-quarters full — and bake for 45 minutes. Allow to cool completely before unmoulding.

♦ This cake keeps well and is delicious served with whipped cream.

INGREDIENTS

To Serve 6

100g/4oz plain chocolate

50g/2oz unsalted butter

3 eggs, separated

50g/2oz caster sugar

1 tsp vanilla sugar

1 dsp flour

50g/2oz ground almonds

Pre-heat the oven to 180°C/350°F/Gas Mark 4.

159

Le Paris-Brest (far left), a
nutty pastry ring filled
with creamy coffee
custard; recipe page 158.
Truffes au Chocolat (left),
chocolate truffles
flavoured with rum;
recipe page 162.
Oranges Glacées Givrées
(below), a refreshing
orange sorbet;
recipe page 174.

Pate a Kugelhopf

A LIGHT TEABREAD WITH RAISINS

(Alsace and Lorraine)

It is said that Queen Marie Antoinette was very fond of this pastry – which contributed a great deal to the fashion then for sweets made from yeast doughs. Some authorities however, believed that it was Carême who popularized this pastry in Paris when he established himself as a pastry cook.

INGREDIENTS

To Serve 6

250g/9oz strong flour

15g/½oz yeast

225ml/7½fl oz milk, warmed

2 eggs

75g/3oz butter

1 tsp salt

25g/1oz caster sugar

120g/4½oz seedless raisins

Pre-heat the oven to 220°C/ 425°F/Gas Mark 7

• *Illustration, page 176*

Sift a quarter of the flour into a bowl and make a well in the centre. Mix the yeast with two-thirds of the warmed milk and pour into the well. Mix in the flour gradually to make a soft, almost liquid, dough and beat well. Sift the remaining flour on top but do not mix in at this stage. Put to rise in a warm place until the yeast dough cracks the flour on the top.

Beat the dough and flour together, adding the eggs one at a time, and enough of the remaining milk to give a soft dough. Beat in the softened butter, salt, sugar and the raisins. Pour into a greased kugelhopf mould — it should only half fill the mould — and put to rise until the mixture reaches the top of the mould.

Bake for 20-30 minutes, remove from the oven, cover for a few minutes with a teacloth — the steam will help to free the kugelhopf easily from the mould — and turn onto a wire rack to cool.

♦ This quantity will fill 2 earthenware kugelhopf moulds, size 8. If the authentic mould is not obtainable, two 18cm/7 inch ring moulds may be used instead.

Truffes au Chocolat

CHOCOLATE RUM TRUFFLES

(Languedoc and the Centre)

INGREDIENTS

Makes approx. 30

225g/8oz plain chocolate

100ml/3½fl oz whipping cream

1 tbsp rum

50g/2oz chocolate vermicelli

• *Illustration, page 161*

Melt the plain chocolate in a basin over a pan of hot water. Place the cream in a small pan, bring to the boil and cool until lukewarm. Remove the chocolate from the heat, add the rum and cream and mix well. Place the mixture in a refrigerator.

When it is beginning to set, beat very well — use an electric mixer if possible — until it becomes creamy and light in colour and texture. Allow to set completely.

Roll teaspoonfuls of the mixture in chocolate vermicelli, coat well and form into neat round shapes. Chill in the refrigerator until firm. Place in paper cases and keep chilled until required.

162

COMPOTE DE POIRES AU VIN ROUGE

PEARS IN RED WINE

(Anjou and the Loire)

Place the wine, sugar and cinnamon stick in a pan, heat gently and stir until the sugar has dissolved. Peel the pears, leaving the stalk on and remove the core from the bottom of each pear with the point of a knife. Place the pears in the hot syrup, cover with a lid and simmer gently until they are tender and translucent.

When the pears are cooked, remove them from the syrup and place on a serving dish. Reduce the syrup by half, pour over the pears and sprinkle with the almonds.

♦ When poaching the pears, choose a small saucepan so the pears can be cooked standing upright and covered by the syrup.

INGREDIENTS

To Serve 4

300ml/½pt red wine

100g/4oz sugar

2.5cm/1 inch piece of cinnamon stick

4 pears

15g/½oz flaked almonds, browned

● *Illustration, page 172*

Preparing the pears. Leave the stalk on and, once peeled, remove the core from the bottom of each pear with the point of a knife.

163

Gâteau Normande, an apple and almond cake, coated with icing; recipe page 167.

164

CREME D'HOMERE

WINE AND HONEY CREAM WITH CARAMEL SAUCE
(Languedoc and the Centre)

INGREDIENTS

To Serve 6

100g/4oz sugar

50ml/2fl oz water

350ml/12fl oz sweet white wine

150g/5oz clear honey

a pinch of cinnamon

a strip of lemon peel

6 eggs

Pre-heat the oven to 160°C/325°F/Gas Mark 3

Place the sugar and water in a small pan and stir over a gentle heat until the sugar has dissolved. Raise the heat and boil the syrup until it turns a rich brown colour — do not stir while it is boiling or the syrup may crystallize. Pour into a 15cm/6 inch charlotte mould or soufflé dish and tilt the mould carefully to coat the sides. The mould will get very hot once the caramel is poured into it so be sure to protect the hands with oven gloves.

Put the wine in a pan with the honey, cinnamon and lemon peel, and heat slowly until the honey has dissolved completely. Allow to cool slightly. Beat the eggs lightly, then pour the honey mixture on to them, whisking all the time, and pour into the caramel lined mould.

Stand the mould in a bain marie and cook for 1~1¼ hours. To test if the mixture is cooked, insert a knife which should come out clean. Allow to cool in the mould and when completely cool, turn out onto a serving dish.

♦ This dessert can be served with Madeleines (see page 183) or Soleils de Nice (see page 179).

TARTE AU CITRON

ALMOND AND LEMON FLAN
(Provence)

INGREDIENTS

To Serve 4-6

2-3 lemons

350g/13oz caster sugar

1 vanilla pod

300ml/½pt water

Pâte sucrée made with 150g/5oz plain flour (see page 69)

1 egg

50g/2oz ground almonds

grated rind of ½ lemon

a few angelica leaves

Pre-heat the oven to 200°C/400°F/Gas Mark 6

• Illustration, page 176. See page 33 for step-by-step illustrations of lining a flan ring

Cut the lemons into very thin slices, place them in a bowl, cover with boiling water and leave to soak for 4 hours or overnight.

Place the lemons and water in a large pan and cook slowly until quite soft, then remove and drain them. Put 300g/11oz of the sugar, the vanilla pod and 300ml/½pt water into a saucepan, add the lemon slices and simmer for 15-20 minutes. Remove the lemon slices with a draining spoon and put them on a plate. Reserve the syrup.

Roll out the Pâte sucrée on a lightly floured board and line into an 18cm/7 inch flan ring.

Mix the egg and remaining 50g/2oz sugar in a bowl, and add the ground almonds and lemon rind. Beat well and pour into the pastry case. Bake for 20-25 minutes.

Reduce the lemon syrup quickly until it is of a thick consistency. When the flan is cooked, brush the top with the lemon syrup and decorate with the lemon slices and angelica leaves. Brush over once again with the lemon syrup and serve cold.

GATEAU NORMANDE

AN APPLE AND ALMOND CAKE WITH A PASTRY BASE

(Normandy)

It is thought that frangipan was invented by an Italian perfumer named Frangipani, who lived in Paris during the reign of Louis XIII.

Wash the apples and cut them into quarters. Remove any blemishes, but do not peel or core. Place them in a saucepan with 2-3 tablespoons of water, cover with a lid and cook over a gentle heat until they are soft. Pass through a sieve, return to a clean pan, add the sugar and cook until a thick purée is obtained. Allow to cool.

Roll out the Pâte sucrée on a lightly floured board and line into a square 15cm/6 inch moule à manqué or cake tin. Prick the base and sides well and cover the base with the puréed apples.

To make the frangipan, place the almonds and sugar in a bowl, add the whole egg and the 2 egg yolks, and mix well. Beat the 2 egg whites stiffly and fold them in lightly with the flour and kirsch. Pour this over the apples, smooth the top and bake for 15 minutes, then reduce the temperature to 180°C/350°F/Gas Mark 4 and bake for a further 35 minutes. Allow to cool in the tin for 15 minutes then turn out carefully onto a wire rack — the pastry base will now be uppermost.

Place all the dry ingredients for the almond paste in a bowl and mix with enough egg white to form a stiff paste. Colour this pale green and make into 12 small apples. Tint them lightly with the carmine colouring to give a realistic appearance. Colour the remaining almond paste a slightly darker green and shape into leaves.

When the base is cold, make the icing. Mix the icing sugar with kirsch, add sufficient water to obtain a coating consistency, and pour over to coat the top and sides. Place 3 almond paste apples and some leaves in each corner and allow the icing to set before serving.

INGREDIENTS

To Serve 6-8

450g/1lb cooking apples

50g/2oz sugar

Pâte sucrée made with 150g/5oz plain flour (see page 69)

Frangipan

90g/3½oz ground almonds

90g/3½oz caster sugar

3 eggs, 2 of them separated

25g/1oz plain flour

2 tbsp kirsch

Almond paste

50g/2oz ground almonds

25g/1oz caster sugar

25g/1oz icing sugar, sifted

a little egg white

a little green colouring

a little carmine colouring

Glacé icing

225g/8oz icing sugar, sifted

1-2 tbsp kirsch

water

Pre-heat the oven to 200°C/400°F/Gas Mark 6.

• *Illustration, page 164*

DESSERTS

167

Crêpes au Miel, honey
and hazelnut pancakes
served with fresh cream;
recipe page 171.

FAR BRETON

A BATTER PUDDING WITH PRUNES

(Brittany)

To Serve 6-8

150g/5oz plain flour

a pinch of salt

100g/4oz sugar

1 tsp vanilla sugar

3 eggs

450ml/¾pt milk

175g/6oz prunes, soaked, cooked and stoned

50g/2oz unsalted butter

Pre-heat the oven to 220°C/ 425°F/Gas Mark 7

Sift the flour and salt into a bowl and mix in the sugar and vanilla sugar. Make a well in the centre, add the eggs and half the milk. Mix together, drawing the flour in gradually from the sides of the bowl, and adding the rest of the milk until a smooth batter is obtained. Stir in the prunes.

Melt the butter in a 1.2lt/2pt fireproof dish, pour in the mixture and cook for 40 minutes or until golden brown. Serve hot or cold.

FRAISES GLACEES CHANTILLY

STRAWBERRIES WITH RASPBERRY PUREE AND CREAM

(Ile de France and the North)

INGREDIENTS

To Serve 4

450g/1lb firm ripe strawberries

225g/8oz raspberries

65g/2½oz icing sugar, sifted

150ml/¼pt Crème Chantilly (see page 71)

3-4 macaroons, finely crushed

• *Illustration, page 156*

Crème Chantilly was created in honour of Le Grand Duc de Condé, cousin of Louis XIV. His chef Vatel committed suicide when there was not enough food for the royal feast.

Hull the strawberries, put them in a serving bowl and stand the bowl in crushed ice. Liquidize the raspberries, and sieve to remove the pips. Add the icing sugar, mix well, and coat the strawberries with the raspberry purée.

Just before serving, pile the Crème Chantilly on top of the strawberries and sprinkle with the macaroons.

KUIGN-AMAN

A RICH BUTTER CAKE

(Brittany)

Sift the flour and salt into a bowl and make a well in the centre. Mix the yeast with 2 tablespoons of the warm water and pour into the well. Add enough water to make a soft and pliable dough, then knead until smooth. Place the dough in a bowl, cover with cling film and leave to rise for 30 minutes.

Place the dough on a lightly floured board and roll to a circle approximately 46cm/18 inches in diameter. Spread with half the butter leaving a 2.5cm/1 inch border. Sprinkle with 50g/2oz of the sugar. Fold the circle in half, then in half again and chill for 10 minutes. Repeat this process once more, using the remaining butter and another 50g/2oz of the sugar.

Carefully roll the dough to a 30cm/12 inch circle, place on a baking sheet, brush with the egg yolk and sprinkle with the remaining sugar. Bake for 30 minutes. Half way through the cooking time, spoon over the butter that has run from the dough.

♦ It is **very important** to have a baking sheet with an edge, so the butter does not run into the oven.

INGREDIENTS

To Serve 4-6

450g/1lb strong flour

½tsp salt

15g/½oz yeast

450ml/¾pt warm water, approx.

225g/8oz butter, softened

175g/6oz caster sugar

1 egg yolk

Pre-heat the oven to 225-250°C/425-450°F/Gas Mark 7-8

CREPES AU MIEL

HONEY AND HAZELNUT PANCAKES

(Franche-Comté)

Sift the flour into a bowl, and make a well in the centre. Add the egg, egg yolk and oil and beat in half of the milk, drawing in the flour from the sides of the bowl. Add the rest of the milk and beat well.

Mix the honey and nuts together, beating well, and stir in the orange rind and Cointreau.

Lightly oil a crêpe or frying pan and heat until very hot. Cover the base of the pan with a thin layer of the batter and cook for 1-2 minutes. Turn the crêpe over and cook the other side. Remove and keep hot. Cook the remaining batter in the same way.

While the crêpes are still hot, spread with a layer of the honey and nut mixture and roll them up. Place in a warm serving dish and serve at once.

♦ These crêpes are delicious served with a jug of fresh cream.

INGREDIENTS

To Serve 4-6

150g/5oz plain flour

1 egg

1 egg yolk

1tbsp oil

300ml/½pt milk

100g/4oz honey

100g/4oz hazelnuts, roasted and ground

grated rind of 1 orange

1tbsp Cointreau

• *Illustration, page 168*

*Compôte de Poires au Vin Rouge
(above), pears in red wine syrup;
recipe page 163.
Cremet d'Angers (right), a light
heart-shaped cream and cheese
dessert, topped with raspberry purée;
recipe page 175.*

Oranges Glacees Givrees

ORANGE SORBET
(Provence)

INGREDIENTS

To Serve 8

11 oranges

juice of 2 lemons

carmine colouring

250g/9oz caster sugar

40ml/1½fl oz kirsch

• *Illustration, page 161*

Wash the oranges and cut a lid from one end of 8 of them. Remove the flesh with a teaspoon, taking care not to tear the shell, and place the shells in the refrigerator to chill. Squeeze the juice from the remaining 3 oranges.

Sieve the orange flesh, and mix in the lemon and orange juices and a little carmine colouring. If there is less than 900ml/1½pt of juice, add water to make up this amount. Add the sugar and dissolve thoroughly. Cool in the refrigerator, add the kirsch and then freeze. (See ♦ below.)

Immediately before serving, fill the orange shells with the sorbet and cover with the lids.

♦ If you have an electric ice cream machine, follow the manufacturer's instructions and when the sorbet is frozen, continue as stated in the recipe.

If this is not available, the sorbet can be frozen very easily using a refrigerator freezing section or freezer as follows. Turn the freezing section or freezer to its lowest setting. Pour the mixture into a shallow metal container and allow to partly set, then remove and whisk well. Repeat this process two or three more times. Use as stated in the recipe.

Mousse au Chocolat et aux Marrons

CHOCOLATE AND CHESTNUT MOUSSE
(Lyonnais)

INGREDIENTS

To Serve 4

225g/8oz plain chocolate

3 tbsp strong black coffee

4 eggs, separated

2 tbsp brandy

50g/2oz sweetened chestnut purée

2 tsp grated plain chocolate

Place the chocolate in a saucepan, add the coffee and melt over a very gentle heat. Add the egg yolks and the brandy to the chocolate, mix for 1-2 minutes over a very low heat and add the chestnut purée, beating it well into the mixture.

~~Bake for 15 minutes or until golden brown. Allow to cool on a wire~~ chocolate mixture, pour into individual dishes and chill well. Decorate with the grated chocolate.

✻ Beat the egg whites very stiffly, fold them carefully into the

CREMETS D'ANGERS

A LIGHT CREAM AND CHEESE DESSERT WITH RASPBERRY PUREE

(Anjou and the Loire)

Line small heart-shaped cremet moulds with muslin. Mix the double and soured creams together and whisk until they are thick. Soften the cheese with enough milk to give a creamy consistency. Whisk the egg whites and salt until they are stiff and fold into the cheese mixture alternately with the whipped creams. Place the mixture in the moulds and leave to drain on a tray overnight.

Liquidize the raspberries, sieve to remove the pips, add the icing sugar and mix well.

Turn out the moulds and arrange on a serving dish, coat with the raspberry purée.

♦ Cremet moulds are heart shaped, made of porcelain or plastic, with holes in the base. If these are not available, use yoghurt or cream pots with holes pierced in the bottom.

The cremets can be served with caster sugar and whipped cream if preferred.

INGREDIENTS

To Serve 6

300ml/½pt double cream

150ml/¼pt soured cream

175g/6oz curd cheese or cream cheese

a little milk

2 egg whites

a small pinch of salt

450g/1lb raspberries

50g/2oz icing sugar, sifted

• *Illustration, page 173*

LES BIARRITZ

WAFER-THIN CHOCOLATE-COATED ALMOND BISCUITS

(Pays Basque)

Place the sugar, vanilla sugar and ground almonds in a bowl and mix with enough unbeaten egg white to form a soft paste. Place teaspoonfuls of the mixture on a greased baking sheet and spread into thin rounds approximately 5cm/2 inches in diameter.

Bake for 15 minutes or until golden brown. Allow to cook on a wire rack and when cold, using a knife, coat the base with the melted chocolate. Sprinkle with the coconut, and leave until quite set before serving.

INGREDIENTS

Makes 30

120g/4½oz caster sugar

1 tsp vanilla sugar

120g/4½oz ground almonds

2-3 egg whites

50-75g/2-3oz plain chocolate, melted

25g/1oz desiccated coconut

Pre-heat the oven to 180°C/350°F/Gas Mark 4

175

Pâte à Kugelhopf (right), a light teabread dotted with raisins; recipe page 162.
Tarte au Citron (below), almond and lemon flan decorated with lemon slices and angelica leaves; recipe page 166.
Tarte aux Pruneaux (far right), a prune flan with redcurrant jelly and wine, covered with apricot glaze, sprinkled with almonds and decorated with cherries; recipe page 179.

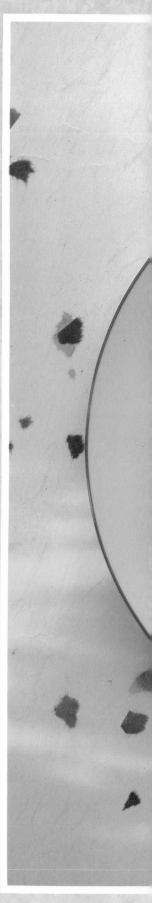

CREPES AUX POMMES DORIN

INGREDIENTS

To Serve 6

For the batter

150g/5oz plain flour

1 egg

1 egg yolk

1 tbsp oil

300ml/½pt milk

1 tbsp Calvados

For the filling

75g/3oz unsalted butter

1kg/2lb cooking apples, peeled, cored and thinly sliced

4 tbsp sugar

2-3 tbsp single cream

40ml/1½fl oz Calvados

To finish

sugar

2-3 tbsp Calvados

PANCAKES WITH APPLES AND CALVADOS

(Normandy)

For the batter, sift the flour into a bowl, make a well in the centre, and add the egg, egg yolk and oil. Beat in half of the milk, drawing in the flour from the sides of the bowl. Add the rest of the milk and the Calvados and beat well.

For the filling, melt the butter in a thick pan and cook the apples, stirring all the time, until they are soft and pulpy. Stir in the sugar, cream and Calvados.

Lightly oil a crêpe or frying pan and heat until very hot. Cover the base of the pan with a thin layer of the batter and cook for 1-2 minutes. Turn the crêpe over to cook the other side. Remove and keep hot. Cook the remaining batter in the same way.

Place a crêpe in the bottom of a hot fireproof dish, spread with some of the apple mixture and cover with another crêpe. Continue in this way sandwiching the apple mixture between each crêpe and finishing with a crêpe on top. Dust thickly with the sugar, heat the remaining Calvados and flame the crêpes with this. Serve at once.

♦ To serve, cut the crêpes into wedges.

TURBAN D'AGEN

INGREDIENTS

To Serve 6

2 leaves of gelatine

225g/8oz large prunes, soaked overnight in 225ml/7½fl oz red wine

2 tbsp apricot jam

100g/4oz pudding rice

600ml/1pt milk

1 vanilla pod

75g/3oz caster sugar

300ml/½pt double cream

A DELICIOUS CREAMY RICE RING WITH A PRUNE AND RED WINE FILLING

(Pays Basque and the South-West)

Brush an 18cm/7 inch ring mould very lightly with oil.

Soak the gelatine in cold water. Place the prunes and wine in a small pan and cook for 8-10 minutes. Remove the stones and mix the prunes with apricot jam.

Place the rice in a pan of boiling water, boil for 5 minutes, drain and rinse under the tap. Place the rice with the milk and vanilla pod in a large pan and cook until the rice is tender and the mixture is thick. Remove the vanilla pod, stir in the sugar and gelatine and allow to cool.

Whisk the cream until if forms soft peaks, fold into the rice mixture and pour into the mould. Chill until firm. Unmould carefully onto a serving dish and fill the centre with the prunes. Serve very cold.

SOLEILS DE NICE

ALMOND PETITS FOURS

(Provence)

These little cakes are supposed to represent the sun shining over Nice.

Put the ground almonds, sugar and vanilla sugar in a bowl, and mix well. Add a level tablespoon of apricot jam and enough unbeaten egg white to form a stiff paste.

Cut into 30 pieces, form into balls and roll in the flour. Brush with beaten egg and coat with the almonds. Place on a baking sheet lined with rice paper and make an indentation in the centre of each with a fingertip.

Bake for 10 minutes, remove and cool on a wire rack and trim off any excess rice paper. Fill each indentation with warmed apricot jam and arrange very small strips of angelica around like the rays of the sun.

INGREDIENTS

Makes 30

100g/4oz ground almonds

100g/4oz caster sugar

½ tsp vanilla sugar

apricot jam

1 egg white

25g/1oz plain flour

a little beaten egg

50g/2oz almonds, browned and chopped

rice paper

angelica

Pre-heat the oven to 190°C/375°F/Gas Mark 5

● *Illustration, page 181*

TARTE AUX PRUNEAUX

A PRUNE FLAN WITH REDCURRANT JELLY AND WINE

(Anjou and the Loire)

Place the prunes and the wine in a pan and cook for 10 minutes. Drain, allow them to cool, remove the stones and mix the prunes with the redcurrant jelly.

Roll out two-thirds of the pastry on a lightly floured board and line into an 18cm/7 inch flan ring. Roll out the remaining pastry to form a lid. Fill the flan case with the prune mixture, moisten the edges of the pastry and cover with the lid, pressing the edges together and trim off the excess pastry. Mark a circle in the centre of the lid with a 2.5cm/1 inch cutter.

Bake for 35-40 minutes or until the pastry is well browned and the base is dry. Remove the circle of pastry from the lid, discard it, and brush the flan all over with the apricot glaze. Sprinkle generously with the almonds and put back into the oven to brown. Remove the flan, allow it to cool, decorate with the cherries and peel, and brush again with apricot glaze.

INGREDIENTS

To Serve 6

225g/8oz large prunes, soaked overnight in 300ml/½pt white wine

100g/4oz redcurrant jelly

Pâte demi-feuilletée made with 225g/8oz plain flour (see page 69)

apricot glaze

1 tbsp chopped almonds

glacé cherries, halved

candied orange peel, cut into crescents

Pre-heat the oven to 220°C/425°F/Gas Mark 7

● *Illustration, page 177. See page 33 for step-by-step illustrations of lining a flan ring*

Madeleines (above), shell-shaped
sponge cakes; recipe page 183.
Soleils de Nice (right), sunshine
desserts coated with almonds;
recipe page 179.

Poires belle dijonnaise

BLACKCURRANT ICE CREAM WITH PEARS AND RASPBERRY PUREE

(Burgundy)

To Serve 6-8

225g/7½fl oz milk

1 vanilla pod

2 egg yolks

175g/6oz sugar

450g/1lb blackcurrants

2-3 tbsp water

300ml/½pt double cream

450g/1lb raspberries

75g/3oz icing sugar, sifted

3 pears, halved and poached in 300ml/½pt sugar syrup

Warm the milk with the vanilla pod and leave for half an hour to infuse. Remove the vanilla pod, then mix the egg yolks and 50g/2oz of the sugar together and stir in the milk. Return to the pan and cook, stirring all the time, until it thickens. Do not allow it to boil. Strain into a large bowl and leave to cool.

Cook the blackcurrants with the water and the remaining sugar until tender, pass through a sieve, cool and add to the custard. Stir in the lightly whipped cream and freeze. (See ♦ below).

Line a round or rectangular cake tin with tin foil and fill with the partly frozen ice cream. Wrap well and place in the freezer.

Liquidize the raspberries, sieve to remove the pips, add the icing sugar and mix well.

Just before serving, turn the ice cream onto a chilled serving dish, arrange the pears on top and coat with the raspberry purée.

♦ If you have an electric ice cream machine, follow the manufacturer's instructions and when the ice cream is partly frozen, continue as stated in the recipe.

If this is not available, the ice cream can be frozen very easily using a refrigerator freezing section or freezer as follows. Turn the freezing section or freezer to its lowest setting. Pour the mixture into a shallow metal container and allow to partly set, then remove and whisk well. Repeat this process two or three more times. Use as stated in the recipe.

Chamonix

MERINGUE NESTS WITH CHESTNUT PUREE AND CREAM

(Franche Comté)

To Serve 6-8

2 egg whites

120g/4½oz caster sugar

225g/8oz can of sweetened chestnut purée

150ml/¼pt double cream

25g/1oz chocolate, finely grated

Pre-heat the oven to 110°C/ 225°F/Gas Mark ¼

Line 2 or 3 baking sheets with non-stick silicone paper.

Beat the egg whites very stiffly, add 1 tablespoon of the sugar and continue beating until the mixture forms stiff white peaks. Fold in the remaining sugar, put the mixture into a piping bag with a 1cm/½ inch plain nozzle, and pipe into flat spirals approximately 5cm/2 inches in diameter. Bake for 1 hour or until the meringues lift easily from the paper. Allow to cool.

Put the chestnut purée into a piping bag with a small plain nozzle and pipe a nest of chestnut purée on the edge of the meringues. Whisk the cream fairly stiffly, place a spoonful in the centre of each nest and sprinkle with the grated chocolate. Serve at once.

Madeleines

SHELL-SHAPED SPONGE CAKES

(Alsace and Lorraine)

Small, light, shell-shaped sponge cakes originally from Commercy in Lorraine which, dipped into a cup of tea, had such great effect in Marcel Proust's A la Récherche du Temps Perdu.

Grease the madeleine tins with melted lard and dust with equal quantities of extra flour and caster sugar.

Put the eggs, sugar and vanilla sugar into a bowl and whisk over a pan of hot water until thick and creamy. Remove from the hot water and continue whisking until cool.

Lightly fold in the sifted flour and then the butter, and spoon the mixture into the madeleine tins. Bake for 15-20 minutes.

♦ It is important that the pan of water is removed from the heat when whisking the eggs and sugars.

INGREDIENTS

Makes 24

2 eggs

50g/2oz caster sugar

1 tsp vanilla sugar

50g/2oz plain flour

50g/2oz butter, melted

Pre-heat the oven to 200°C/ 400°F/Gas Mark 6

● *Illustration, page 180*

Tarte au fruit a L'ALSACIENNE

FRUIT AND CUSTARD FLAN

(Alsace and Lorraine)

Roll out the Pâte brisée on a lightly floured board, line into an 18cm/7 inch flan ring and prick the base well. Bake blind for approximately 10 minutes or until the pastry is dry and firm.

If using plums or apricots, halve the fruit and remove the stones. For cherries, remove the stones by using a cherry stoner or by cutting in half.

Poach the fruit gently with the sugar and water until just tender. Do not allow the fruit to break up.

Fill the flan with the poached fruit and bake for 5 minutes. Mix the egg with the cream, pour this over the fruit and bake for a further 10 minutes. Dust with the icing sugar and serve warm.

INGREDIENTS

To Serve 6

Pâte brisée made with 100g/ 4oz plain flour (see page 71)

450g/1lb fruit — plums, apricots or cherries

50g/2oz sugar

150ml/¼pt water

1 egg

4 tbsp double cream

1 tbsp icing sugar, sifted

Pre-heat the oven to 190°C/ 375°F/Gas Mark 5

● *See page 33 for step-by-step illustrations of lining a flan ring*

CLASSICS

By definition, a classic recipe should be one that has not been altered in any way since it was first created, but there will always be slight differences of opinion as to the true appearance and flavour of a dish. We hope that our classic recipes are true interpretations of the originals, and while remaining true in spirit to them are also concise, easy to follow and not over-elaborate.

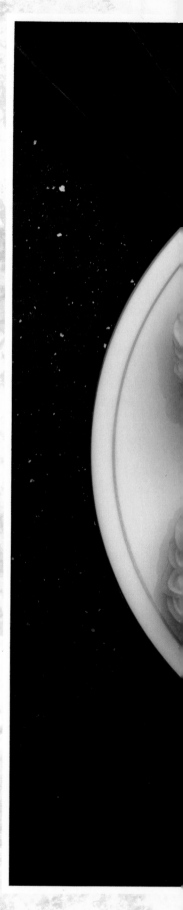

Coquilles Saint Jacques à la Côte d'Argent, a delicious combination of scallops, prawns and mushrooms served in white wine sauce and surrounded by swirls of creamy potato; recipe page 187.

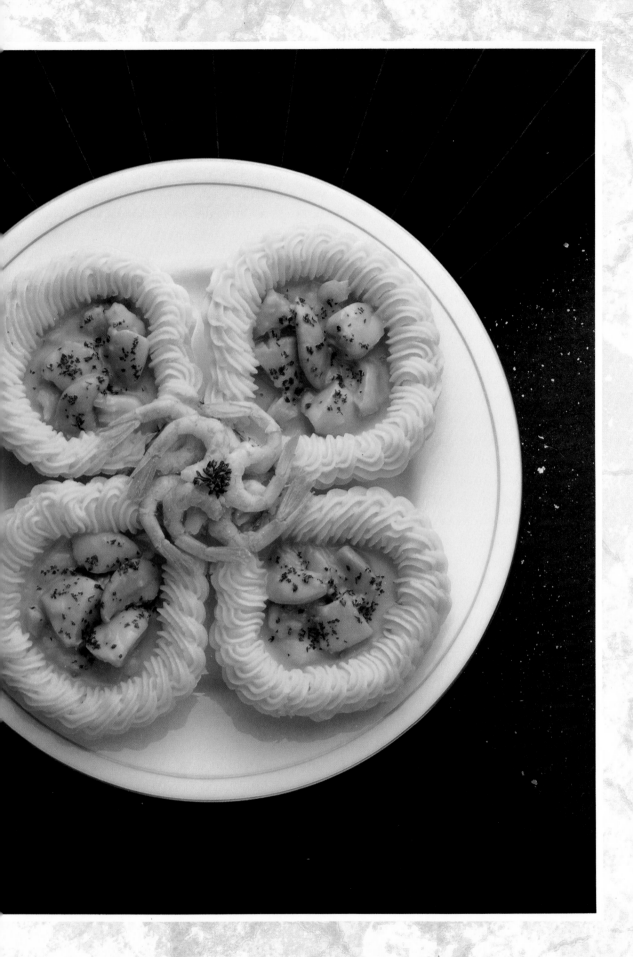

CONSOMME JULIENNE

INGREDIENTS

To Serve 4-6

350g/12oz shin of beef

1.2lt/2pt brown stock (see page 68)

1 carrot, finely chopped

1 leek, finely chopped

1 stick of celery, finely chopped

bouquet garni

1 tomato, quartered

salt

black pepper

4 egg whites

120ml/4fl oz water

2 tbsp sherry

julienne strips of carrot, turnip and French beans

• *Illustration, page 201*

CLEAR SOUP WITH VEGETABLE GARNISH

Remove the fat and shred the meat finely. Place in a pan with the stock, vegetables, bouquet garni, tomato, salt and black pepper and the egg whites lightly beaten with the water. Bring slowly to simmering point, stirring all the time. When it begins to cloud, stir very gently until it boils.

Reduce the heat and simmer for 20-30 minutes until a crust has formed and the liquid is clear and brilliant. Strain through a clean muslin cloth into a perfectly clean bowl. Add the sherry and the julienne strips and pour into a warmed tureen.

♦ Great care must be taken not to mix the crust with the liquid when straining the consommé or the result will be cloudy. All utensils must be clean and grease free.

POTAGE AU CRESSON

INGREDIENTS

To Serve 4

2 bunches of watercress

50g/2oz butter

900ml/1½pt vegetable stock (see page 68)

2 large potatoes, thinly sliced

salt

black pepper

300ml/½pt milk

3 egg yolks

300ml/½pt single cream

• *Illustration, page 201*

CREAM OF WATERCRESS SOUP

Wash and dry the watercress. Reserve 12 small sprigs for the garnish and chop the remainder roughly. Melt the butter in a large saucepan, add the watercress and sweat it for 10 minutes. Do not allow it to burn. Add the stock, potatoes, salt and black pepper. Bring to the boil, cover the pan with a lid and simmer for 25 minutes. Put through a fine sieve or liquidize, return to the pan which has been rinsed out, pour in the milk and reheat.

Mix the egg yolks and cream, pour a little of the soup onto this mixture, then return to the pan and heat through carefully—it must not boil. Taste and adjust the seasoning. Pour into a warmed tureen or soup bowls and garnish with the sprigs of watercress.

CREME VICHYSSOISE

LEEK AND POTATO SOUP

This soup was invented by a French chef in New York in 1917 and it is often served chilled. Sometimes the title is shortened to Vichyssoise alone.

Clean the leeks and slice thinly into rings. Melt the butter in a fairly large pan, add the potatoes, leeks, salt and black pepper, cover with a lid and sweat them until tender. Pour in the chicken stock and simmer for 20 minutes.

Remove from the heat, put through a fine sieve or liquidize, add the cream, taste and adjust the seasoning. Reheat and sprinkle with the chopped chives.

♦ This soup may be served hot or chilled.

INGREDIENTS
To Serve 6

8-10 small leeks

50g/2oz butter

3-4 medium potatoes, thinly sliced

salt

black pepper

1.2lt/2pt white chicken stock (see page 68)

300ml/½pt single cream

3-4 tbsps finely chopped chives

COQUILLES SAINT JACQUES A LA COTE D'ARGENT

SCALLOPS, PRAWNS AND MUSHROOMS IN A WHITE WINE SAUCE WITH PIPED POTATO

The scallop shell is the symbol of St James and in the Middle Ages, pilgrims journeying to his shrine in Northern Spain would have the symbol embroidered on their cloaks. The French, therefore, called them Coquilles St Jacques.

Cut the scallops into 3 or 4 pieces, place them in a pan with the white wine, shallot, bouquet garni, salt and black pepper, and poach for 5 minutes.

Melt the butter in a small pan and cook the mushrooms until soft. Add the shelled prawns, taste and adjust the seasoning. Put a spoonful of this mixture in the bottom of the scallop shells and cover with the scallops. Keep hot.

Strain the liquor in which the scallops were poached into a clean pan, reheat and whisk in sufficient Beurre manié to make a coating sauce. Taste and adjust the seasoning and simmer for 2-3 minutes.

Pour the sauce over the scallops and sprinkle with the parsley and garlic. Pipe a border of Pommes de terre duchesse round the edge of the scallop shells and garnish with the whole prawns.

INGREDIENTS
To Serve 4

4 scallops, cleaned

150ml/¼pt dry white wine

1 shallot, finely chopped

bouquet garni

salt

black pepper

25g/1oz butter

100g/4oz mushrooms, chopped

50g/2oz shelled prawns

Beurre manié (see page 65)

1 tbsp finely chopped parsley

1 tsp finely chopped garlic

Pommes de terre duchesse (see page 71)

4 whole prawns

• Illustration, page 184

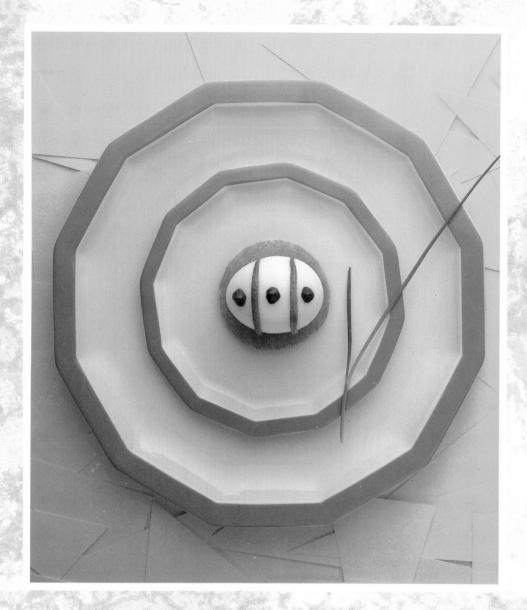

Croissants (above right), tasty
crescent-shaped butter rolls;
recipe page 215.
Oeufs Tonnelier (above), eggs filled
with anchovy mixture and decorated
with anchovy fillets and capers;
recipe page 190.
Crabe Garni (right), dressed crab
served in its shell; recipe page 191.

189

Oeufs Tonnelier

ANCHOVY-STUFFED EGGS

INGREDIENTS

To Serve 4

4 hardboiled eggs

4 anchovy fillets, finely chopped

black pepper

50g/2oz butter

4 round croutes 6cm/2½ inches in diameter (see page 52)

To finish
anchovy fillets
capers

• *Illustration, page 189*

Cut the eggs in half lengthwise and remove the yolks carefully. Mix yolks with the anchovy fillets, black pepper and the softened butter. Fill one-half of each egg with the mixture and cover with the second half, fitting it neatly on the top.

Spread the remaining mixture on the croûtes, making a slight hollow in each to allow the egg to rest securely. Place an egg on each croûte, and decorate with 2 strips of anchovy fillets and 3 capers to imitate the hoops on a barrel. Serve cold.

Mayonnaise d'Homard

LOBSTER MAYONNAISE

There is a great debate about the origins of the name mayonnaise. It is possible that it is related to the siege of Port Mahon in Minorca in 1756.

INGREDIENTS

To Serve 4

225g/8oz cooked new potatoes, finely diced

600ml/1pt Sauce mayonnaise made with tarragon vinegar (see page 66)

white pepper

a few drops of tabasco sauce

4 tomatoes

2 cooked lobsters, about 750g/1½lb each

paprika

1 tsp chopped chives

½ round lettuce, washed and dried

watercress, washed and dried

2 hardboiled eggs, quartered

• *Illustration, page 192. See page 40 for step-by-step illustrations of dressing lobster.*

Mix the potatoes with some of the mayonnaise — this should be of a coating consistency. Season with salt and white pepper. Add the tabasco sauce to the remaining mayonnaise.

Cut the tomatoes in half, remove the pips, sprinkle the inside with salt and turn upside down to drain.

Place each lobster on a chopping board with the tail spread out flat. Hold the head firmly in one hand and with a strong sharp knife push the point firmly into the cross on the top of the head. Bring the knife down through the tail splitting it in two, turn the lobster and split through the head in the same way. Remove the sac in the head — behind the eyes — and the intestine which runs in a black line through the meat near the tail. Remove the gills — dead mens' fingers — and the shell to which they are adjoined.

Lift out the flesh from the shells, cut into slanting slices and return these to the opposite shell from which they were taken so that the red side is uppermost. Crack the claws, remove the flesh, place this in the head shells and coat with some of the mayonnaise. Dust with paprika.

Dry the tomatoes on kitchen paper, fill with the potato and sprinkle with the chives.

Place the lobster halves on a serving dish. Garnish with the lettuce, small bunches of watercress, hardboiled eggs and the tomatoes. Serve any remaining mayonnaise separately.

CRABE GARNI

DRESSED CRAB

Remove the large pincers and claws and open the crab by pressing firmly on the tail end. Remove the body from the shell of the crab. Discard the gills — dead mens' fingers — and the stomach sac behind the eyes. Remove the brown flesh from the shell and put it into a basin. Remove the white flesh from the pincers, claws and body and put in a separate basin — the body of the crab may be cut in half and the white flesh removed with a skewer. Mix the brown flesh with the breadcrumbs, vinegar, salt and black pepper. Add the cream and some salt and black pepper to the white meat.

Scrub the shell thoroughly, dry on kitchen paper and break off the edge of the shell at the natural marking. Brush the shell with a little oil and place the brown meat in the centre and the white meat on either side. Cover the white meat with the egg white and the brown meat with the egg yolk. Place a line of parsley down the joins. Serve on a bed of lettuce.

INGREDIENTS

To Serve 1-2

1 crab

1 tbsp white breadcrumbs

1 tsp wine vinegar

salt

black pepper

1-2 tbsp double cream

oil

1 hardboiled egg, separated: white, very finely chopped; yolk, sieved

parsley, finely chopped

a few lettuce leaves

• *Illustration, page 189. See page 41 for step-by-step illustrations of dressing crab.*

CANARD A L'ORANGE

ROAST DUCK WITH ORANGE

Prick the skin of the duck, sprinkle with salt and cover with the butter. Place the duck in a roasting pan with the carrot and onion, cover with foil and cook for 20 minutes per 450g/1lb plus 20 minutes extra. Remove the foil for the last 30 minutes to allow the skin to brown.

Peel the zest from 2 of the oranges, cut it into fine julienne strips and blanch in boiling water for 5 minutes or until tender. Remove the skin and pith from these 2 oranges and cut the fruit into segments, retaining any juice. Cut strips from the rind of the third orange with a canelle knife and slice the orange thinly. Squeeze the juice from the fourth orange.

Remove the duck from the roasting pan, cut off the wing tips and place the duck on a serving dish. Pour off the excess fat from the roasting pan, add the Sauce demi-glace and the orange juice to the pan and stir well. Reheat the sauce, strain, add the julienne strips, taste and adjust the seasoning. Pour the sauce over the duck and arrange the orange segments down the back of the bird. Garnish the edge of the dish with the orange slices.

◆If preferred, the duck may be carved for serving. Cut off the legs and divide into two. Remove each breast from the carcass and cut in two. Arrange the joints on a serving dish, pour over the sauce and garnish with the oranges.

INGREDIENTS

To Serve 4

1.75-2.25kg/4-5lb duck, trussed

salt

25g/1oz butter

1 carrot, quartered

1 onion, quartered

4 oranges

300ml/½pt Sauce demi-glace, unstrained (see page 65)

black pepper

Pre-heat the oven to 200°C/ 400°F/Gas Mark 6

• *See page 47 for step-by-step illustrations of trussing*

Mayonnaise d'Homard, a succulent lobster mayonnaise accompanied by stuffed tomatoes and garnished with lettuce, small bunches of watercress and hardboiled eggs; recipe page 190.

POULET EN CHAUDFROID

BONED STUFFED CHICKEN GLAZED WITH ASPIC

Chaudfroid was created by accident. When the Maréchal de Luxembourg was called away to a meeting of the King's council, his hot fricassée of chicken became cold. He ate the dish on his return and so enjoyed it that it became a favourite.

INGREDIENTS

To Serve 8-10

1.5-1.75kg/3½-4lb chicken

450g/1lb round of sweet cure ham

For the stuffing
225g/8oz veal, minced

225g/8oz pork, minced

1 egg

1 large onion, finely chopped

75g/3oz breadcrumbs

2 tbsp brandy

2 tbsp sherry

1 tbsp chopped parsley

½ tsp chopped thyme

salt

black pepper

For poaching
1 onion

2 carrots

1 stick of celery

1 leek

bouquet garni

Chaudfroid sauce
75g/3oz butter

75g/3oz flour

900ml/1½pt chicken stock

8 leaves of gelatine

1.5lt/2½pt aspic jelly (see page 67)

150ml/¼pt double cream

For the decoration
red pepper

lemon peel

cucumber peel

tarragon

● *Illustration, page 197. See page 44 for step-by-step illustrations of boning a chicken*

Starting at the neck end of the chicken, with a sharp knife remove the wishbone, then scrape away the flesh from the rib cage, easing where necessary with the fingers until the wing joint is reached. With great care scrape the flesh away from the wing bone up to the first joint and then cut carefully through the joint. Repeat with the other wing. Continue down the rib cage, paying special attention when scraping near the ridge of the breast bone and on the underside of the keel — in order not to puncture the skin — turning back the flesh while scraping until the leg joint is reached. Scrape away the flesh from the thigh bone until the first joint is reached — for a better shape the drumstick is left in place but can be removed if required — and cut carefully through the joint. Repeat with the other leg. Continue to scrape the flesh away from the bone structure until the whole carcass can be easily removed.

Cut the ham in half and put the halves together to form a semi circle.

Mix all the ingredients for the stuffing together and season with salt and black pepper.

Sew up the vent opening of the chicken and any splits in the skin. Place the ham inside the chicken with the rounded side under the breast and fill the rest of the cavity evenly with the stuffing. Sew the neck flap to cover the stuffing. Truss the legs in place, tie the chicken in a muslin cloth to keep its shape, and weigh it.

Place the chicken in a pan with the poaching vegetables and the bouquet garni, cover with water, bring to the boil and simmer for 20 minutes per 450g/1lb plus 20 minutes extra. Cool in the stock, remove and drain well. Refrigerate until required and when completely cold remove the muslin and strain the stock.

Melt the butter for the sauce in a pan, remove from the heat, add the flour, return to the heat and cook for 2-3 minutes, stirring all the time. Add the measured stock, bring to the boil and simmer for 4-5 minutes. Dissolve 6 leaves of the gelatine in 225ml/7½fl oz of aspic and add to the sauce. Pass through a fine sieve or muslin, stir in the cream and leave to set.

Dissolve the remaining 2 leaves of gelatine in 300ml/½pt aspic and leave to set. When completely set, chop on a piece of damp greaseproof paper.

Prepare the decoration. Using an aspic cutter, cut petal shapes from blanched pepper or lemon peel and cut a stalk and leaves from cucumber peel or blanched tarragon. Arrange to form a large flower design.

Place the chicken on a wire rack over a bowl and coat with the Chaudfroid sauce — which must be on the point of setting — and leave until completely set. Dipping each piece in some liquid aspic, carefully transfer the decoration to the breast of the chicken. Leave the decoration to set, then spoon over a layer of aspic which must be on the point of setting. Allow to set completely, arrange on a serving dish and garnish with the chopped aspic.

♦To melt down aspic jelly, heat in a bowl over hot water, stirring gently until the aspic becomes liquid.

Bouchees a la reine

PUFF PASTRY CASES FILLED WITH CHICKEN AND MUSHROOM

The bouchée was created for Marie Leszcinska, gourmet queen of Louis XV.

Roll out the puff pastry on a lightly floured board to a 33cm/13 inch square. Cut out 16 circles 7.5cm/3 inches in diameter. Brush lightly with the beaten egg. With the back of a small knife, mark the circles with a lattice pattern and cut the centres neatly from 8 of them with a 4.5cm/1¾ inch cutter. Place the whole circles on a dampened baking sheet, put a circle with its centre removed on each one and press down firmly. Place in a refrigerator to chill for 20 minutes.

Bake for 15-20 minutes, then carefully remove the round of pastry that rises through the centre and keep this for a lid. With a teaspoon, scoop out any soft pastry from inside the bouchées. Reduce the temperature to 190°C/375°F/Gas Mark 5 and return the bouchées to the oven for 5-7 minutes to dry out. Reserve the lids until the bouchées are filled.

Melt half the butter in a small pan, add the flour and cook for 3-4 minutes. Remove from the heat and stir in the stock a little at a time. Bring to the boil stirring all the time and cook for a further 4-5 minutes.

Heat the remaining butter in a clean pan, and add the mushrooms, lemon juice, salt and black pepper. Cook until tender and drain well. Add the mushrooms and chicken to the sauce, reheat, taste and adjust the seasoning.

Fill the bouchées with the mushroom and chicken mixture, replace the lids and serve hot.

INGREDIENTS

To Serve 4

Pâte feuilletée made with 225g/8oz strong flour (see page 70)

beaten egg to glaze

50g/2oz butter

25g/1oz flour

300ml/½pt chicken stock

50g/2oz mushrooms, thinly sliced

1 tsp lemon juice

salt

black pepper

225g/8oz shredded cooked chicken

Pre-heat the oven to 230°C/450°F/Gas Mark 8.

• *See page 30 for step-by-step illustrations of how to make Pâte feuilletée.*

195

Savarin (above), a light
rum-flavoured yeast sponge cake
decorated with almonds and glacé
cherries; recipe page 214.
Poulet en Chaudfroid (right), boned
chicken stuffed with a mixture of pork
and veal and glazed with aspic;
recipe page 194.

Marquise Alice, a praline
and cream dessert with
chocolate cones;
recipe page 212.

198

Bavarois Rubane (left), a colourful layered dessert with three flavours; recipe page 213.
Consommé Julienne (below), clear soup with vegetable garnish; recipe page 186.
Potage au Cresson (far left), a cream of watercress soup, garnished with a sprig of watercress; recipe page 186.

201

Sole Colbert, deep fried
sole served with lemon and
parsley butter;
recipe page 206.

204

Ris de Veau Guizot (left), braised
veal sweetbreads served with deep
fried potato puffs, tomatoes and
olives; recipe page 209.
Crème Opéra (above), a caramel
custard with strawberries and cream;
recipe page 211.

Poulet Archiduc

CHICKEN IN A CREAMY SAUCE WITH PORT AND BRANDY

INGREDIENTS

To Serve 4-6

50g/2oz butter

1.5kg/3½lb chicken, jointed

salt

black pepper

3 tbsp white port

2 tbsp brandy

150ml/¼pt Sauce béchamel (see page 66)

150ml/¼pt double cream

350g/12oz asparagus, cooked and tossed in butter

• See page 46 for step-by-step illustrations of jointing a chicken

Heat the butter in a heavy pan and lightly brown the chicken joints. Season with salt and black pepper, cover with greaseproof paper and a lid and cook slowly for 30 minutes. Place the chicken joints on a serving dish and keep warm.

Add the port and brandy to the pan, stir well, then add the Sauce béchamel and the cream. Allow to simmer for 3-4 minutes, remove from the heat, taste and adjust the seasoning. Pour the sauce over the chicken and garnish with the asparagus. Serve at once.

Sole Colbert

DEEP FRIED SOLE WITH LEMON AND PARSLEY BUTTER

INGREDIENTS

To Serve 4

4 sole, 225-350g/8-12oz each

a little milk

seasoned flour

2-3 eggs, beaten with 1 tbsp oil

white breadcrumbs

Beurre maître d'hôtel
100g/4oz butter

2 tbsp finely chopped parsley

juice of ½ lemon

salt

black pepper

oil for deep-frying

• Illustration, page 202. See page 39 for step-by-step illustrations of preparing sole.

This dish is named after Jean Baptiste Colbert, who was a Chief Minister of Louis XIV.

For the Beurre maître d'hôtel, beat the butter well until it is of a creamy consistency, then add the parsley and the lemon juice a little at a time. Season with salt and black pepper to taste. Shape into a roll 2.5cm/1 inch in diameter on damp greaseproof paper and chill.

Remove the fins and the dark and white skins from the sole. Leave the heads on. With the dark skinned side uppermost, run the filleting knife down the backbone and raise the fillets at each side, cutting almost to the edge. Roll them back but do not remove. Snip the backbone at each end and in the centre so it may be removed after cooking.

Dip each sole into the milk, then the seasoned flour, and coat with the beaten egg and breadcrumbs—it is important that the fillets remain rolled back during this process. Cook the sole in hot deep fat (180°C/350°F) until golden brown and drain well on kitchen paper. Remove the backbones from the fish and place on a hot serving dish.

Arrange slices of Beurre maître d'hôtel down the centre of the fish just before serving.

FILETS DE SOLE BONNE FEMME

POACHED SOLE WITH SAUCE HOLLANDAISE

Skin the fish fillets and fold each one in half with the skin side inside. Place the fillets in a shallow fireproof dish with the carrot, onion, bouquet garni, salt and black pepper. Pour over the wine, cover with buttered greaseproof paper and poach in the oven for 15-20 minutes.

Place the mushrooms in a small pan with the butter, lemon juice and some salt and black pepper. Cover with greaseproof paper and a lid and cook gently for 5-7 minutes or until tender.

For the sauce hollandaise, put 2 tablespoons of the liquor in which the fish was cooked into a pan and reduce by half. Strain onto the lightly beaten egg yolks. Mix well, place the bowl over a pan of hot water and whisk continuously until a thick creamy custard consistency is obtained. Beat in the butter a little at a time. Do not allow the sauce to get too warm or it may curdle. When all the butter has been added, stir in the lemon juice and season with salt and white pepper. Stir in the mushrooms and the parsley. Keep warm.

Strain the remaining fish liquor into a clean pan and reduce it quickly until only 2 tablespoons remain. Add this to the Sauce hollandaise. Place the fish fillets in a hot serving dish, coat with the sauce and put under a very hot grill until the top is lightly browned— this must be done very quickly.

INGREDIENTS

To Serve 4

8 fillets of sole

1 carrot, sliced

1 onion, sliced

bouquet garni

salt

black pepper

300ml/½pt dry white wine

100g/4oz button mushrooms, sliced

25g/1oz butter

2 tsp lemon juice

2 tbsp finely chopped parsley

Sauce hollandaise
2 egg yolks

100g/4oz unsalted butter

2 tsp lemon juice

salt

white pepper

Pre-heat the oven to 180°C/ 350°F/Gas Mark 4

See page 39 for step-by-step illustrations of preparing sole

Preparing the sole. Run a filleting knife down the backbone and roll the fillets back, ready for coating.

ff333

TOURNEDOS HENRI IV

FILLET STEAK WITH A BUTTER AND HERB SAUCE

Henry IV — Henry of Navarre — was King of France and a great hero of Béarn. Béarnaise sauce was created in St Germain around 1830.

For the Sauce béarnaise, place the peppercorns, shallot and vinegar in a small pan and reduce by half. Add the stock and strain into a bowl holding the lightly beaten egg yolks. Mix well, place the bowl over a pan of hot water and whisk continuously until the eggs thicken. Beat in the butter a little at a time. Do not allow the sauce to get too warm or it may curdle. When the butter has been added, stir in the tarragon, taste and season with salt and black pepper. Put the sauce into a piping bag with a small rosette nozzle.

For the Pommes de terre pont-neuf, cut the potatoes into 6cm/$2\frac{1}{2}$ inch lengths, 1cm/$\frac{1}{2}$ inch wide x 1cm/$\frac{1}{2}$ inch thick — it is important that the potatoes are of a uniform size — then dry them on kichen paper. Blanch for 7-8 minutes in hot oil in a deep fat pan (160°C/325°F). Remove the chips from the pan and raise the temperature to 190°C/375°F, replace the chips and cook for 2-3 minutes or until golden brown. Drain well on kitchen paper and sprinkle with salt.

Heat the butter in a heavy pan, and fry the tournedos allowing 1-2 minutes on each side, according to their thickness. Place each tournedos on a croûte, arrange on a hot serving dish and pipe a ribbon of Sauce béarnaise around the top of each. Arrange the potatoes in the centre of the dish and garnish with sprigs of watercress.

INGREDIENTS

To Serve 4

40g/1½oz butter

4 tournedos

4 croûtes 7.5cm/3 inches in diameter (see page 52)

watercress

Sauce béarnaise

6 peppercorns, lightly crushed

1 shallot, finely chopped

2 tbsp tarragon vinegar

1 tbsp white stock (see page 68)

2 egg yolks

100g/4oz unsalted butter

1 tbsp finely chopped tarragon

salt

black pepper

Pommes de terre pont-neuf

6 large potatoes

oil for deep-frying

RIS DE VEAU GUIZOT

BRAISED VEAL SWEETBREADS WITH A GARNISH OF DEEP FRIED POTATO PUFFS, TOMATOES AND OLIVES

Soak the sweetbreads in cold water for 1-2 hours. Put them in a pan, cover with cold water, bring to the boil and blanch them for 1-2 minutes. Drain and refresh in cold water. Trim the sweetbreads and remove the fat and membranes.

If using calf's sweetbreads, put between 2 plates, place a heavy weight on the top and leave until quite cold.

Thread a larding needle with fine strips of bacon fat and lard the sweetbreads with this. This does not apply if using lamb's sweetbreads because they are too small.

Melt 50g/2oz of the butter in a heavy pan, add the carrots, onion, celery, salt and black pepper and stir well until they are coated with the butter. Place the sweetbreads on top of the vegetables and add the bouquet garni. Stir the tomato purée into the stock and pour over the sweetbreads together with the wine and brandy. Sprinkle with the mint, cover with greaseproof paper and a lid, and cook for 30 minutes.

For the Pommes de terre à la dauphiné, mix the Pommes de terre duchesse and Pâte à choux well together, and season with salt and black pepper. Place in a piping bag with a 1cm/$\frac{1}{2}$ inch plain nozzle and pipe 2cm/1 inch lengths into hot deep fat (180°C/350°F), cutting them off with a sharp knife. When golden brown, remove and drain well. If the potato mixture disintegrates during frying it is too soft. This can be corrected by beating in a little flour.

Put a knob of the remaining 25g/1oz butter on each tomato and cook them for 5-10 minutes in the oven.

Remove the sweetbreads from the pan, and arrange on a serving dish. Strain the liquor in which they were cooked and add the arrowroot slaked with a little cold water. Bring to the boil and cook for 2-3 minutes until it thickens slightly. Taste and adjust the seasoning and pour over the sweetbreads.

Heat the olives in the melted butter. Arrange the Pommes de terre à la dauphine at each end of the dish, the tomatoes and olives at each side and sprinkle the sweetbreads with the parsley.

INGREDIENTS

To Serve 4-6

750g/1$\frac{1}{2}$lb calf's (or lamb's) sweetbreads

larding bacon

75g/3oz butter

3 carrots, sliced

1 onion, sliced

1 stick of celery, sliced

salt

black pepper

bouquet garni

1 tsp tomato purée

150ml/$\frac{1}{4}$pt white veal stock (see page 68)

150ml/$\frac{1}{4}$pt dry white wine

2-3 tbsp brandy

1 tbsp finely chopped mint

Pommes de terre à la dauphiné made with Pommes de terre duchesse (see page 71) and Pâte à choux made with 50g/2oz strong flour (see page 69)

oil for deep-frying

4 tomatoes, skinned

1 tsp arrowroot

10 stuffed olives

1 tbsp melted butter

parsley, finely chopped

Pre-heat the oven to 190°C/375°F/Gas Mark 5.

• *Illustration, page 204*

CHARLOTTE MONTREUIL

INGREDIENTS

To Serve 6

4 leaves of gelatine

300ml/½pt milk

3 egg yolks

25g/1oz sugar

1 tsp vanilla sugar

150ml/¼pt peach purée

2 tbsp maraschino

225ml/7½fl oz double cream

50g/2oz peaches, thinly sliced

Biscuits à la cuillère

3 eggs, separated

75g/3oz caster sugar

90g/3½oz plain flour

1 tsp vanilla sugar

icing sugar, sifted

To finish

a few peach slices

4 tbsp double cream

Pre-heat the oven to 180°C/ 350°F/Gas Mark 4

A MOULDED DESSERT OF PEACHES AND CREAM COVERED WITH SPONGE FINGER BISCUITS

The fruits of the Paris orchards have a great reputation, and some of the most famous are the peaches of Montreuil. The dessert known as a charlotte was invented by the great chef Carême when he was chef to Czar Alexander I.

For the Biscuits à la cuillère, line 2 or 3 baking sheets with strips of greaseproof paper 15cm/6 inches wide.

Put the egg yolks and sugar in a bowl and beat until thick and light in colour — the mixture should hold its shape for the count of three when a trail is drawn. Whisk the egg whites until stiff and fold them into the creamed mixture lightly, alternately with the sifted flour and vanilla sugar. Place in a piping bag with a plain 1cm/½ inch nozzle and pipe 13cm/5 inch lengths onto the greaseproof paper. Dust with the finely sifted icing sugar and tap off the surplus. Bake for 10-13 minutes or until pale golden brown. Remove from the oven, turn the paper upside down on a wire rack and tear the paper away from the biscuits immediately — this must be done while the biscuits are still hot. Allow to cool.

Place a circle of greaseproof paper in the base of a 15cm/6 inch charlotte mould.

Trim the sides of the sponge finger biscuits and cut off 1cm/½ inch from one end. Line the sides of the mould with the sugared side of the biscuits against the mould and the cut end on the base — it is important that the biscuits fit tightly so none of the filling can seep through. If necessary, use a tiny dab of butter on every second or third biscuit to help them stick.

Soak the gelatine in cold water.

Warm the milk in a small pan. Put the egg yolks, sugar and vanilla sugar in a bowl and mix well. Pour on the milk, return to the pan and stir over a gentle heat until the custard thickens without boiling. Remove from the heat and stir in the gelatine. Strain into a clean bowl, add the peach purée and maraschino and leave to cool, stirring occasionally. When the custard is on the point of setting, fold in the lightly whisked cream. Put half the mixture into the lined mould and place over ice until this has set. Cover with the thinly sliced peaches and then pour on the remaining mixture. Allow to set in a refrigerator.

Trim the biscuits to the level of the custard and turn out onto a serving dish. Remove the greaseproof paper and decorate with the peach slices. Whisk the cream until stiff, place in a piping bag with a small rosette nozzle and pipe cream around the edge.

♦ Drained canned peaches may be used for the purée or, if preferred, skinned fresh peaches may be used in which case you may need to add more sugar to the custard.

CREME OPERA

A CARAMEL CUSTARD WITH STRAWBERRIES AND CREAM

Place 100g/4oz of the sugar and the water in a small pan and stir over a gentle heat until the sugar has dissolved. Raise the heat and boil the syrup until it turns a rich brown colour — do not stir while it is boiling or the syrup may crystallize. Pour into a 1lt/1¾pt ring mould and tilt the mould carefully to coat the sides. The mould will get very hot once the caramel is poured into it so be sure to protect the hands with oven gloves.

Warm the milk with the vanilla pod and leave to infuse for half an hour. Put the eggs, egg yolks and remaining sugar in a bowl and mix well. Add the milk and strain into the caramel lined mould. Stand the mould in a bain marie and cook for 40-45 minutes. To test if the custard is cooked, insert a knife which should come out clean. Allow to cool completely, preferably overnight.

Loosen the edge of the custard by easing it away from the mould with the fingertips. Turn out onto a serving dish. Whisk the cream until stiff and place half in a piping bag with a small rosette nozzle. Fold the crushed meringues into the remaining cream and put in the centre of the custard. Arrange the strawberries around the centre and edge of the custard and pipe stars of cream over the meringue and cream mixture. Serve very cold.

INGREDIENTS

To Serve 6

200g/7oz sugar

150ml/¼pt water

450ml/¾pt milk

1 vanilla pod

2 eggs

4 egg yolks

150ml/¼pt double cream

3-4 meringue shells, crushed

225g/8oz large strawberries, macerated in 2 tbsp kirsch

Pre-heat the oven to 180°C/350°F/Gas Mark 4

• Illustration, page 205

Lining the ring mould. Protect your hands with oven gloves. Pour the hot caramel into the mould and turn the mould around until it is completely coated.

Marquise Alice

INGREDIENTS

To Serve 6

3 leaves of gelatine

300ml/½pt milk

4 egg yolks

40g/1½oz sugar

600ml/1pt double cream

50g/2oz crushed Praline (see page 71)

5-6 sponge finger biscuits

4 tbsp kirsch

50g/2oz plain chocolate

1-2 tbsp redcurrant jelly

• *Illustration, page 198.*

A PRALINE AND CREAM DESSERT WITH CHOCOLATE CONES

The origin of the name praline — a sugared almond — dates from the time of Louis XIII. The Duc de Choiseul-Praslin once offered his favourite mistress a new sweet — a sugared almond. So popular did these sweets become that they were called prasline, and a confectionery shop was opened especially to sell them.

Chill a 19cm/7½ inch moule à manqué or deep sandwich tin.

Soak the gelatine in cold water. Warm the milk in a small pan. Put the egg yolks and sugar in a bowl and beat well. Pour on the milk, mix well, return to the pan and cook gently, stirring all the time, until the custard coats the back of a spoon. Add the gelatine and strain into a clean bowl. Leave until on the point of setting.

Whisk half the cream lightly and when the custard is ready, fold in the cream together with the Praline. Pour some of the mixture into the chilled mould, and cover with the sponge finger biscuits dipped in kirsch, keeping them away from the sides of the mould. Cover with the rest of the mixture, smooth over the top and put in a refrigerator until set and firm.

Melt the chocolate in a bowl over a pan of hot water. Line the inside of 8 cream horn tins with small triangles of greaseproof paper, and coat these with the melted chocolate. Allow to set, and when firm, unmould and cut down to the required size — about 7.5cm/3 inches long — with a pair of scissors.

Loosen the edge of the custard by easing it away from the mould with the fingertips. Dip the mould into hot water for 2-3 seconds and turn out onto a serving dish. Whisk the remaining cream until it forms soft peaks and spread two thirds over the top and sides of the custard. Whisk the remaining one-third until stiff and place in a piping bag with a small rosette nozzle.

Bring the redcurrant jelly to the boil and whisk until smooth. Place in a small piping bag with a very fine plain nozzle and pipe parallel lines about 2.5cm/1 inch apart across the cream on top of the custard. Using the point of a small knife or a thin skewer, quickly draw across the lines of redcurrant jelly in alternate directions to give a feather design.

Decorate the top and base of the custard with some of the cream. Fill 6 chocolate cones with the remaining cream and decorate with a swirl of redcurrant jelly. Arrange cones around base of custard.

♦ 8 cones are made to allow for breakages.

BAVAROIS RUBANE

A LAYERED DESSERT WITH THREE FLAVOURS

Chill a 13cm/5 inch charlotte tin. Melt the chocolate in a bowl over a pan of hot water. Soak the gelatine in cold water.

Warm the milk in a small pan. Put the egg yolks, sugar and arrowroot in a bowl and mix well. Pour on the milk, return to the pan and stir over a gentle heat until the custard thickens without boiling. Remove from the heat and stir in the gelatine.

Divide the custard into three portions. Add the melted chocolate to one portion, the vanilla sugar to the second and the kirsch to the third. Colour the third pink with the carmine. Leave until on the point of setting. Whisk the cream until it forms soft peaks and fold a third of it into each portion of custard.

Put the pink kirsch-flavoured custard in the mould and place over ice until this has set. Cover with the vanilla-flavoured custard and leave to set as before. Finally, cover with the chocolate custard and chill until required.

Loosen the edge of the bavarois by easing it away from the mould with the fingertips. Dip the mould into hot water for 2-3 seconds and turn out onto a serving dish.

INGREDIENTS

To Serve 4-6

100g/4oz chocolate

5 leaves of gelatine

600ml/1pt milk

6 egg yolks

75g/3oz sugar

a pinch of arrowroot

4 tsp vanilla sugar

4 tbsp kirsch

carmine colouring

300ml/½pt double cream

• *Illustration, page 201*

OEUFS A LA NEIGE

POACHED MERINGUES WITH A CUSTARD SAUCE

Whisk the egg whites until they are stiff and fold in 100g/4oz of the sugar and the vanilla sugar. Heat the milk in a deep frying pan, bring to simmering point and, using 2 tablespoons, form the egg whites into egg shapes and drop into the milk. Poach for about 8-10 minutes or until firm, then remove and drain on kitchen paper.

Put the egg yolks, arrowroot and the remaining sugar into a bowl and mix well. Pour on 300ml/½pt of the milk used for poaching the meringues, return to a clean pan and stir over a gentle heat until it thickens without boiling. Remove from the heat, strain into a shallow dish and place the meringues on top. Serve very cold.

INGREDIENTS

To Serve 4

3 eggs, separated

165g/5½ oz caster sugar

1 tsp vanilla sugar

600ml/1pt milk

a pinch of arrowroot

SOUFFLE ROTHSCHILD

A HOT SOUFFLE WITH CRYSTALLIZED FRUITS AND KIRSCH

INGREDIENTS

To Serve 4-6

300ml/½pt milk

1 vanilla pod

50g/2oz butter

50g/2oz plain flour

75g/3oz caster sugar

3 egg yolks

4 egg whites

100g/4oz crystallized fruits, chopped and macerated in 3 tbsp kirsch

5 fresh strawberries or glacé cherries rolled in caster sugar

Pre-heat the oven to 200°C/400°F/Gas Mark 6

Warm the milk with the vanilla pod and leave to infuse for half an hour. Use a little extra butter to grease an 18cm/7 inch soufflé dish and dust it with extra caster sugar.

Melt the butter in a pan, remove from the heat and stir in the flour. Return to the heat and cook for 2-3 minutes, stirring all the time. Remove from the heat, and add the milk a little at a time. Bring to the boil, stirring continuously, and cook for 5 minutes. Remove the pan from the heat and stir in the sugar and the whisked egg yolks. Allow to cool, then fold in the stiffly whisked egg whites.

Spread a thick layer of this mixture in the bottom of the prepared dish and cover with the crystallized fruits and kirsch. Place the rest of the mixture on top and cook for 20-25 minutes. Just before serving, place the strawberries or the glacé cherries on the top and serve immediately.

SAVARIN

A LIGHT RUM FLAVOURED YEAST SPONGE

INGREDIENTS

To Serve 6-8

Lard for greasing

225g/8oz strong flour

200g/7oz sugar

½ level tsp salt

15g/½oz yeast, mixed with 2 tbsps lukewarm water

3 eggs

65g/2½oz butter, melted

450ml/¾pt water

3 tbsps rum

apricot glaze

6-8 almonds, blanched and halved

3 glacé cherries, halved

Pre-heat the oven to 220°C/425°F/Gas Mark 7.

• Illustration, page 196

The savarin was originally known as 'Brillat Savarin' after the gastronome, ambassador and philosopher of the same name (born in Belley in 1755).

Brush a 1lt/1¾pt ring mould with melted lard.

Sift the flour, 25g/1oz of the sugar and the salt into a warm bowl, make a well in the centre and pour in the dissolved yeast and the eggs. Beat well to make a fairly liquid dough and add the cooled melted butter. Beat again until smooth and shiny. Cover and leave in a warm place until it has doubled in size.

Knock back the dough and place in the mould. Leave the dough to rise until it reaches the top of the mould, then bake for 30-40 minutes. Remove from the oven and cover for a few minutes with a teacloth. The steam will help to free the savarin easily from the mould.

Place the remaining sugar and the water in a pan, bring to the boil and simmer for 5 minutes. Add the rum and soak the savarin with this syrup. Place on a serving dish and brush carefully with apricot glaze and decorate with the almonds and glacé cherries.

CROISSANTS

CRESCENT ROLLS

Croissants are not French in origin. When the Turks encircled Budapest ready to attack in 1686, the bakers who were working in the quiet of the early morning to prepare the day's bread heard the Turks trying to tunnel their way through the city wall. The bakers raised the alarm and saved their city. To commemmorate the occasion they created the croissant — to represent the crescent shape of the emblem on the Turkish flag. The rolls won their way to France where they quickly found popularity.

Sift the flour, sugar and salt onto a pastry board, make a well in the centre, and put in the yeast and 2 tablespoons of the water. Mix the yeast and water together with the fingertips, add the remaining water and gradually draw in the flour until it forms a soft dough — it may be necessary to add a little extra water. Place the dough in a bowl, cover with cling film and leave to rise until it has doubled in size. Put to chill in a refrigerator for 2-3 hours or overnight (the dough may be frozen at this stage).

Place the dough on a lightly floured board and roll into a circle 25cm/10 inches in diameter. Soften the butter by tapping it with a rolling pin on a piece of greaseproof paper to elongate it, cut in half, put the two pieces of butter together and repeat until the butter is pliable but still cold. Reform to a rectangle approximately 10 x 15cm/4 x 6 inches. Place the butter in the middle of the dough and fold over the dough from the right and left to cover the butter — it should overlap by about 2.5cm/1 inch. Fold the top and bottom ends to overlap in the same way. Seal the joins with the rolling pin and roll the dough to a rectangle approximately 36 x 18cm/14 x 7 inches. Mark the dough lightly into three. Fold the bottom third up to cover the middle third and the top third down. Seal the edges lightly with the rolling pin, give the dough a quarter turn so the join is now to the right-hand side, and repeat the rolling and folding. Chill the dough for 15 minutes. Roll and fold the dough twice more — giving four rollings and foldings in all — and chill for a further 15 minutes.

Roll the dough to a rectangle 20 x 56cm/8 x 22 inches and trim 5mm/¼ inch from each edge. Cut into 5 triangles with an 18cm/7 inch base and form the sixth triangle from the two end pieces of dough. Place a thin strip of the trimming along the base of each triangle and fold the dough over this. Roll to the point of the triangle and form into horseshoe shapes. Place on a dampened baking sheet and leave to prove in a warm place — it is important not to allow the dough to get *too* hot, as the butter will run from it — until the croissants have doubled in size.

Brush with the beaten egg and bake for about 15 minutes or until golden brown.

INGREDIENTS

Makes 6

225g/8oz strong flour

15g/½oz sugar

½tsp salt

15g/½oz yeast

150ml/¼pt lukewarm water to mix, approx.

100g/4oz butter, chilled

beaten egg to glaze

Pre-heat the oven to 230°C/ 450°F/Gas Mark 8

• *Illustration, page 188. See pages 34~35 for step-by-step illustrations.*

COOKERY TERMS

BAIN MARIE *A roasting pan or similar, containing boiling water, in which food can be cooked gently, separated from direct heat, or kept warm.*

BAKE BLIND *To line an uncooked pastry case with greaseproof paper and fill with dried beans to prevent the pastry from shrinking at the sides or rising on the base. When the pastry is partly cooked, the paper and beans are removed and the pastry is returned to a cooler oven to finish drying out.*

BARD *To tie fat bacon or pork fat round the breast of poultry, game or any lean meat to keep the food moist while cooking.*

BASTE *To spoon pan juices, fat or cooking liquid over the food during cooking to prevent the surface of the food from drying out.*

BEURRE MANIE *Equal quantities of butter and flour worked together to a smooth paste, and used as a thickening for sauces, etc.*

BLANCH *(i) To pre-cook food briefly, usually vegetables, either in boiling water (red or green peppers), or in hot deep fat (potatoes for Pommes de terre pont neuf). (ii) To place in boiling water to remove skins (almonds).*

BOUQUET GARNI *A bunch of herbs tied together with string and used for flavouring stews etc. Parsley stalks, a sprig of fresh thyme and a bay leaf are always used, and are removed after cooking. Other herbs or flavourings such as a celery stalk may be added according to the dish.*

DEGLACER *The addition of liquid — water, stock, wine, brandy, etc. — to very hot juices, fat or sediment on the bottom of the cooking pan. Stirring vigorously while boiling loosens the juices and forms an emulsion to be used as a sauce.*

FARCE *A stuffing for meat, fish, vegetables, etc.*

FLAME *To pour spirit that has been set alight over food.*

FLORETS *Small pieces of cauliflower broken off the main stalk.*

GLACE DE VIANDE *Brown stock reduced to a syrupy consistency used for flavouring and colouring.*

GRATINER *To brown the top of a dish coated with cheese, breadcrumbs or a sauce under the grill or in the top of a hot oven. Sometimes a dish prepared in this way is referred to as 'au gratin'.*

JULIENNE *Small strips of fruit and vegetables approximately the size of a matchstick, used as a garnish.*

To LARD *To thread pieces of bacon fat through very lean meat, poultry or game. A special needle is used with a claw-like end.*

LARDONS *Small strips cut cross-wise from a rasher of bacon.*

LIAISON *A binding or thickening added to sauces, soups, etc. at the end of the cooking time. Egg yolks, cream, beurre manié or blood may be used.*

MACERATE *To soak fresh, crystallized or dried fruit in syrup, wine, spirit or liqueur.*

MARINADE *An acidic mixture containing flavouring and herbs in which meat, game and fish are soaked before cooking to tenderize and improve the flavour. The liquid is often used in the finished dish.*

MARINATE *The verb relating to the above.*

MIREPOIX *The foundation of diced vegetables for a braised dish.*

PURÉE *A thick smooth mixture obtained from food by sieving, liquidizing or blending in a food processor.*
REDUCE *To boil a liquid to reduce it by evaporation, thus intensifying the flavour. (The original liquid must not have been over-seasoned.)*
REFRESH *To pour cold water over vegetables after cooking to preserve the colour and prevent further cooking in their own steam.*
ROUX *Melted butter to which flour has been added, the basis of a sauce.*
SWEAT *To cook food — usually vegetables — very gently in melted fat so that the fat is absorbed and the flavour is drawn from the vegetables. This process prevents a layer of fat flowing on the top of the finished dish. The food should be covered with greaseproof paper and the lid of the pan to prevent steam from escaping.*
VANDYKE *To decorate fruit and vegetables with a zig-zag pattern.*
ZEST *The coloured outside skin of a citrus fruit removed without any pith.*

WEIGHTS AND MEASURES

N.B. In this book, teaspoons, dessertspoons and tablespoons are heaped unless otherwise stated. A pinch is generally as much as can be held between thumb and forefinger.

OVEN TEMPERATURE GUIDE

	ELECTRICITY		GAS MARK
	°C	°F	
Very cool	110	225	¼
	120	250	½
Cool	140	275	1
	150	300	2
Moderate	160	325	3
	180	350	4
Moderately hot	190	375	5
	200	400	6
Hot	220	425	7
	230	450	8
Very hot	240	475	9

LINEAR MEASURES

METRIC	IMPERIAL
3 mm	⅛ inch
5 mm	¼ inch
1 cm	½ inch
2 cm	¾ inch
2.5 cm	1 inch
4 cm	1½ inches
5 cm	2 inches
6 cm	2½ inches
7.5 cm	3 inches
9 cm	3½ inches
10 cm	4 inches
13 cm	5 inches
15 cm	6 inches
18 cm	7 inches
20 cm	8 inches
23 cm	9 inches
25 cm	10 inches
28 cm	11 inches
30 cm	12 inches
33 cm	13 inches

SOLID MEASURES

METRIC	IMPERIAL
10 g	$\frac{1}{4}$ oz
15 g	$\frac{1}{2}$ oz
20 g	$\frac{3}{4}$ oz
25 g	1 oz
40 g	$1\frac{1}{2}$ oz
45 g	$1\frac{3}{4}$ oz
50 g	2 oz
65 g	$2\frac{1}{2}$ oz
75 g	3 oz
90 g	$3\frac{1}{2}$ oz
100 g	4 oz ($\frac{1}{4}$ lb)
120 g	$4\frac{1}{2}$ oz
150 g	5 oz
165 g	$5\frac{1}{2}$ oz
175 g	6 oz
185 g	$6\frac{1}{2}$ oz
200 g	7 oz
225 g	8 oz ($\frac{1}{2}$ lb)
250 g	9 oz
275 g	10 oz
300 g	11 oz
350 g	12 oz ($\frac{3}{4}$ lb)
375 g	13 oz
400 g	14 oz
425 g	15 oz
450 g	16 oz (1 lb)
500 g	$1\frac{1}{4}$ lb
750 g	$1\frac{1}{2}$ lb
	$1\frac{3}{4}$ lb
1 kg	2 lb
	$2\frac{1}{4}$ lb
1.25 kg	$2\frac{1}{2}$ lb
	$2\frac{3}{4}$ lb
1.5 kg	3 lb
	$3\frac{1}{4}$ lb
	$3\frac{1}{2}$ lb
1.75 kg	4 lb
	$4\frac{1}{4}$ lb
2 kg	$4\frac{1}{2}$ lb
	$4\frac{3}{4}$ lb
2.25 kg	5 lb
	$5\frac{1}{4}$ lb
2.5 kg	$5\frac{1}{2}$ lb
	$5\frac{3}{4}$ lb
2.75 kg	6 lb
3 kg	7 lb
3.5 kg	8 lb
4 kg	9 lb
4.5 kg	10 lb

LIQUID MEASURES

METRIC	IMPERIAL
1 × 1.25 ml spoon (or pinch)	$\frac{1}{4}$ teaspoon (or pinch)
1 × 2.5 ml spoon	$\frac{1}{2}$ teaspoon
1 × 5 ml spoon	1 teaspoon
1 × 15 ml spoon	1 tablespoon
$1\frac{1}{2}$ × 15 ml spoons	$1\frac{1}{2}$ tablespoons
2 × 15 ml spoons	2 tablespoons
3 × 15 ml spoons	3 tablespoons
4 × 15 ml spoons	4 tablespoons
5 × 15 ml spoons	5 tablespoons
6 × 15 ml spoons	6 tablespoons
25 ml	1 fl oz
50 ml	2 fl oz
65 ml	$2\frac{1}{2}$ fl oz
85 ml	3 fl oz
100 ml	$3\frac{1}{2}$ fl oz
120 ml	4 fl oz
135 ml	$4\frac{1}{2}$ fl oz
150 ml	5 fl oz ($\frac{1}{4}$ pint)
175 ml	6 fl oz
200 ml	7 fl oz ($\frac{1}{3}$ pint)
225 ml	$7\frac{1}{2}$ fl oz
250 ml	8 fl oz
275 ml	9 fl oz
300 ml	10 fl oz ($\frac{1}{2}$ pint)
350 ml	12 fl oz
400 ml	14 fl oz
450 ml	15 fl oz ($\frac{3}{4}$ pint)
475 ml	16 fl oz
500 ml	18 fl oz
600 ml	20 fl oz (1 pint)
750 ml	$1\frac{1}{4}$ pints
900 ml	$1\frac{1}{2}$ pints
1 litre	$1\frac{3}{4}$ pints
1.2 litres	2 pints
1.25 litres	$2\frac{1}{4}$ pints
1.5 litres	$2\frac{1}{2}$ pints
1.6 litres	$2\frac{3}{4}$ pints
1.75 litres	3 pints
2 litres	$3\frac{1}{2}$ pints
2.25 litres	4 pints

INDEX

219

D

E

F

G

Q

R

S

ACKNOWLEDGEMENTS

We wish to thank all those who helped us prepare this book, in particular Kerenza Harries who assisted us with the preparation of the food for photography.

The publishers wish to acknowledge the kind assistance of *The Reject China Shop*, Beauchamp Place, London for loaning china, *Elizabeth David Ltd*, Goding Street, London for loaning kitchen equipment, *Culpepers Ltd*, Hadstock Rd, Linton, Cambridge for supplying fresh herbs and *Osborne & Little*, Kings Road, London for supplying marbled wallpapers.

PHOTOGRAPHY

All photographs by
Paul Forrester except:

J. Allan Cash Ltd pages 7, 8, 9, 10, 14, 15, 16, 17, 18 and 19

Alastair Campbell page 11

John Wyand page 60